Sleep Sou~~...~~

Volume I

Supercharge Retirement Income

Don't Outlive Your Money!

How to Invest for

More Gain with Lower Risk

Dr. John W Dowdee

ISBN-13:
978-1508499497

ISBN-10:
1508499497

Prolog

I retired in 2008 and like many of you, I was gripped with fear and anxiety when the market crumbled. I knew that I could not live off the meager fraction of a percent that I received from "safe" Certificate of Deposits (CD). Over the long run, I knew I would need higher returns from my investments. I did not want to outlive my money but I could not afford to lose my retirement stake. I was frozen with indecision!

I am a retired engineer with a PhD in mathematics. So I thought, maybe I could devise a way to supercharge my retirement income while lowering my investment risk. After much analysis, I came up with a strategy for constructing what I called the "Sleep Soundly Portfolio". In this book, I share what I have learned along the way. The strategy is based firmly on the mathematical principles of finance but don't worry, you do not need to know math to be successful. In fact, I have gone to great lengths to write a simple, easy to implement plan that is easy to understand without prior knowledge of math or complex finance theory.

I wrote this book for the do-it-yourself investor, who plans to personally manage his nest egg. By doing it yourself, you should be able to "Sleep Soundly" because you know that your investments are in "good hands". Although the book was written with retirees in mind, it is suitable for all ages of investor. In fact, the best way to ensure a comfortable retirement is to start early with a sound investment plan.

The Supercharge Retirement Income strategy is not about a one-size-fits-all portfolio. Instead, you will build a portfolio that is uniquely suited to your specific needs. I will show you how to assemble a diversified portfolio that provides the returns you need at a risk you can live with.

Here are some of the things you will learn:

Chapter 1. We're not in Kansas anymore. As Dorothy said in the Wizard of Oz, "Toto, I've a feeling we are not in Kansas anymore." Well, the stock market has definitely left Kansas. It is no longer the quiet and comfortable environment that greeted your parents and grandparents. This chapter describes how the investment landscape has changed and discusses the impact of the Federal Reserve and High Frequency Trading. This will set the stage for building a portfolio that recognizes the "new normal".

Part I: Fundamentals of Developing a Higher Return, Lower Risk Portfolio.   Chapters 2 through 8 cover what you need to know to construct a diversified portfolio that will provide higher returns at lower risk. Sound impossible? Not really! Markowitz discovered how to achieve this more than 50 years ago and won the Nobel Prize for his pioneering work.

Chapter 2. Stocks, Bonds, and Mutual Funds. This chapter provides a quick tutorial on what you need to know about the traditional methods of investing.

Chapter 3: Exchange Traded Funds (ETFs). Over the last couple of decades, an alternative to traditional mutual funds has emerged and has revolutionized the way people invest. This innovation was called an Exchange Traded Fund (ETF). Like all investments, there are advantages and disadvantages of investing in ETFs. This chapter will provide the insights you will need to determine whether ETFs are right for you.

Chapter 4. Closed End Funds (CEFs). CEFs are one of the best kept secrets on Wall Street. This chapter will discuss how CEFs provides excellent income without excessive risk.

Chapter 5: Understanding Futures. You will likely never trade futures directly as part of your portfolio. However, many ETFs give you access to markets that were once the province of future traders. These specialized ETFs can provide valuable diversification for your portfolio. This chapter provides the fundamental knowledge you will need to invest successfully in these types of ETFs.

Chapter 6. Understanding Call Options. Wall Street cloaks options with an air of complexity but the truth is that options are a simple tool that can actually lower risk. This chapter provides a basic tutorial on how call options work and how you might use them as part of your investment strategy. In particular, the chapter will introduce the concept of "covered calls", which will be expanded upon in Chapter 9.

Chapter 7. Evaluating Risk versus Reward. The key to profitable investing is to balance risks and rewards. In other words, you should make sure that you are adequately compensated for any risks that you are taking. This chapter describes a systematic way of judging the potential reward and risks of your investments.

Chapter 8. Asset Allocation and Diversification. Asset allocation is one of the most critical decisions you can make when developing your investment strategy. Diversification is a key ingredient for managing risks. This chapter provides an easy to understand tutorial on Markowitz's amazing discovery relating how to reduce portfolio risk without sacrificing return.

Part II. Exploring Nontraditional Assets to Spice Up Your Portfolio. Chapters 9 through 14 provide an overview of some of the more nontraditional asset classes that can be used to diversify your portfolio.

Chapter 9. Covered Call Funds. A covered call is a way to receive additional income by sacrificing some of the upside potential of a stock. The risks versus rewards of covered call funds are investigated in this chapter.

Chapter 10. Real Estate Investment Trusts (REIT) Funds. REITs have long been a favorite asset class for income oriented investors. This chapter provides a review of available REIT funds in terms of risks versus rewards.

Chapter 11. Master Limited Partnership (MLP) Funds. The number of MLPs has exploded lately and MLP funds provide an easy way to invest in this relatively complex structure. The risks and rewards associated with MLPs are covered in this chapter.

Chapter 12. Commodity and Agricultural Funds. Commodities and agriculture products run hot and cold but when this asset class takes off, it can soar. This chapter reviews commodity and agricultural funds and evaluates the recent risk and rewards for this class of investments

Chapter 13. Precious Metal Funds. Most investors are familiar with the phenomenal rise of gold that was followed by an equally impressive collapse. This chapter reviews bullion and mining stock funds and how they have fared recently.

Chapter 14. Currency Funds. Most investors have never considered investing in currencies even though ETFs now make it easy to obtain exposure. Currency trading far exceeds the trading volume on all the world's stock exchanges combined! This chapter reviews the risk and rewards associated with currencies from different countries.

Part III How To Construct a Sleep Soundly Portfolio. Chapters 15 to 17 show you how to construct a portfolio that is geared to your reward and risk profile.

Chapter 15. Sleep Soundly CEF Portfolio. This chapter constructs an example high income portfolio using Closed End Funds (CEFs). The portfolio provided a yearly income of about 7% to 8% while beating the S&P 500 on a risk adjusted basis.

Chapter 16. Sleep Soundly ETF Portfolio. This chapter constructs a low risk portfolio using Exchange Traded Funds (ETFs). This portfolio minimized risk while outperforming the S&P 500 on a risk-adjusted basis.

Chapter 17. Parting Thoughts. A few parting thoughts and a discussion of where you can find additional information on the Web.

I understand that the objectives of this book may seem farfetched, especially since Wall Street has perpetuated the myth that retail investors from Main Street cannot manage their own funds. Of course, they want you to trust them and pay them a management fee. After you read this book, I hope you never be intimidated by Wall Street again.

This is the first volume in the Sleep Soundly Portfolio series. The sequel to this book should be published soon and will discuss techniques on how to actively manage risk.

Thank you for purchasing this book. I hope it will provide the insights you need to develop your own unique portfolio that is not only profitable but will also allow you to "sleep soundly" every night.

Table of Contents

Dr. John Dowdee

Chapter 1
We're Not in Kansas Anymore

If you are a stock investor, the first decade of the millennium was dismal to say the least. The stock bull market that began in the 1980s, made stock investing and portfolio management appear easy—all you had to do was buy a basket of blue chip stocks and hold them. The 1990s delivered a whopping 17.6% average annual return. This was the highest return for any decade since 1950. Making money could not have been easier.

Then the new millennium started and a whole new ballgame began. Stock prices (especially tech stock) had reached the stratosphere. Few, if any, of the market pundits foresaw that the bottom was about to fall out—in fact, the new year of 2000 was met with enthusiasm and experts were predicting that we would soon see the Dow over 30,000. But on March 10, 2000, the bubble burst. On that day, the NASDAQ was at 5,132, more than double what it had been only a year before. The NASDAQ began a long steep descent into the depths of despair, finally bottoming at about 1114 in September, 2002. All the other major market indexes also had steep declines. During the bear market, about 5 trillion dollars of market value evaporated.

As the stock market collapsed, investors searched for alternative investments and found promising candidates in real estate. Interest rates were low and down payments were also low so the baby boomers moved in mass into real estate investments. The number of homes bought for "investment" jumped 50%. Then the quants at the banks and investment houses figured out a way to slice and dice mortgages to supposedly reduce the risk of subprime lending. A new bubble was born and the market took off again. The DOW blasted upward, reaching a new high at 14,198 on October 11, 2007. As with all bubbles, this one burst and by March 9, 2009, the DOW had fallen over 54% to 6,443! Thus in 2009, the DOW was at about the same level it was in 1997! A whole 12 years had passed with zero return from the stock market—talk about a lost decade!

The bull began roaring again in 2009, with the market increasing over 300% by the middle of 2014. As I write this book in late 2014, the market has made new all-time highs and the bull appears to be strong. Is this the start of a decade long bull market like the 1980s and 1990s or will the market roll over and take back the gains? The reality is that no one knows the future. Yes some people are more informed guessers than others but at the end of the day, they are all guessing.

Instead of guessing, you should listen to the market and tune out the hype. The market action provides better advice than any guru on television. All you have to do is interpret what the market is telling you. This book will help you improve your listening ability.

The Buy and Hold strategy that was so successful in the 1990s may not be dead but it is on life support. No longer can you count on receiving a reasonable gain from the stock market just by passively holding a basket of stocks. For over a decade, a buy-and-hold strategy has not rewarded the investor and has caused significant pain along the way.

To survive in the "new normal" each investor needs to take charge of his own portfolio and perform some active asset allocation. You don't need to be a day trader but you do need to monitor your investments and take action when required. This book will help you make informed decisions by pointing out assets that have an excellent reward to risk profile.

We're not in Kansas Anymore!

As Dorothy said in the Wizard of Oz, "Toto, I've a feeling we are not in Kansas anymore." Well, the stock market has definitely left Kansas. The investment environment in the new millennium is vastly different from the go-go years of the 1980s and 90s. Prices are being manipulated by forces that were not even imagined even a few years ago. Three of the drivers that make this market different are discussed below.

Federal Reserve Activism

In response to the economic collapse of 2007, the Federal Reserve embarked on an unprecedented path of activism. In December of

2008, they instituted the first round of Quantitative Easing (QE1) by committing to purchase $600 billion dollars of Mortgage Backed Securities (MBS). The idea was to stimulate the economy by printing more money to purchase financial assets. The specific goal of QE1 was to drive down mortgage interest rates to stimulate the housing market, which had fallen like a rock. Before QE1 ended in March 2010, another $750 billion was spent on MBSs plus another $300 billion on treasury bills.

QE2 was initiated in November, 2010, a few months after QE1 ended. The idea was to drive down long term interest rates by buying long term treasuries. Overall, $600 billion dollar was spent on this idea.

A new twist was tried after QE2 ended in June 2011. This initiative was termed Operation Twist and was touted to be a way of stimulating the economy without printing more money. In this rendition, the Fed sold short term treasuries (less than 3 year maturity) and used the proceeds to buy long term treasuries (6 to 30 years). The objective again was an attempt to stimulate the housing market and other investments by keeping long term rates low. Initially the Fed allocated $400 billion to this effort but later this was increased by another $267 billion.

All these efforts had limited success. The economy stayed sluggish, the unemployment rate refused to go down, and the housing market had only a minor recovery. So in September, 2012, the Fed launched QE3. The idea was to purchase $40 billion dollars of MBS each month, until the economy began to improve. Since there was no specified end date, this is sometimes called QE Forever or QE Infinity. In December, 2012, the Fed upped the ante by adding $45 billion a month to purchase long term treasuries.

Thus, the Fed has committed to buy $85 billion a month of securities until the economy improves. With this amount of money flooding the markets, it was difficult for the market to go down substantially. Some of the techniques for predicting the market are no longer working because the Fed actions have substantially altered the supply and demand statistics that use to provide clues to market direction.

As this is being written in late 2014, Fed Chairman Ben Bernanke has been replaced by Janet Yellen and the Fed has embarked on tapering the amount of asset purchases. The hope was that the Fed could unwind the quantitative easing in such a way not to upset the economy or the stock market. Quantitative Easing officially ended in October, 2014 with the promise to keep interest rates low. Time will be the judge if the Fed objective were achieved. However, after experiencing Fed intervention for more than 7 years, it will be a long time before the market returns to "normal".

High Frequency Trading (HFT)

HFT typically uses computer algorithms to decide when to buy or sell. The main difference between HFT and other forms of trading is speed. I don't mean just fast, I mean extraordinarily fast, like thousands of transactions per second! The profit made on a single transaction can be measured in pennies or even fractions of a penny. But when you multiply the small profit by millions of transactions, you get "real money". In 2012, HFT accounted for more than half the stock exchange volume on a daily basis and in that year, HFT generated more than 21 billion of dollars in profits (that's Billions with a "B")!

The HFT algorithms are typically not developed by economists. They are developed by science nerds using exotic math that is executed on supercomputers.

Some say that HFT plays a critical role by providing liquidity to the market. However, if the HFT algorithms decide to stop buying for a few seconds, then watch out! HFT trading was one of the main reasons for the Flash Crash that occurred at 2:47 PM EST on May 6, 2010. At that time, bids dried up. Within seconds, the Dow Jones Industrial average plunged more than 1,000 points, only to recover a few minutes later.

The regulators are trying to implement rules that will prevent Flash Crashes in the future. Hopefully they will be successful, but regardless, HFT is here to stay. As an individual investor, you have to be very careful when using Stop Loss orders you set with your broker. If another flash crash occurs, many of your stops could be hit and your positions sold at prices well below your stop loss point. In the Flash Crash of 2010, some stocks went from $20 per share to pennies in just a few seconds. To avoid this, you should use "mental stops" or if you must use brokerage stops, consider using Stop Limit orders. These do not provide as much protection as normal stops but they will assure you sell at the limit prices. There is no free lunch so you must balance risk management with your other market strategies.

Hedge Funds

Hedge Funds are privately managed funds. They are not sold to the general public so they are freed from many of the regulations that govern mutual funds. To invest in a hedge fund, you must be an "accredited investor", which means that you need a net worth of more than a million dollars (excluding the value of your home) or you have made over $200,000 a year for the last two years. If you qualify, then you can invest in a hedge fund, but the fees are not cheap. Most hedge funds charge a fixed management fee of 2% plus they receive 20% of your profits. Hedge funds were originally started to reduce risks but today, most try to maximize return on investment (which also maximizes their fees).

Like HFTs, hedge funds are typically based on complex mathematical algorithms but unlike HFT, hedge funds have a longer time horizon. Hedge funds have become popular with the top earners and the funds now have more than 2 trillion dollars under management!

Hedge funds have had some spectacular successes like George Soros who amassed a net worth of more than 19 billion as a hedge fund manager. Or take James Simon. He was a math whiz who founded the Renaissance Technologies hedge fund and now has a net worth of more than $11 billon. The current star is David Tepper, whose Appaloosa Management hedge fund has returned more than 30% per year since it was founded in 1993. Truly amazing!

But don't think that hedge funds always make money. They have also had some monumental blowups. One of the most famous is Long Term Capital Management (LTCM) that had 2 Nobel laureates on the Board of Directors. LTCM made some bad bets on Russian currency and lost more than $4 billion dollars when Russia defaulted. The collapse of LTCM precipitated a market crisis that could have been much worse had not the Fed and some large banks came to their rescue.

But the losses by LCTM paled in comparison to Morgan Stanley, where a trader lost more than $9 billion in 2007! Then there was Amaranth Advisors, where one of their employees lost over $6 billion dollars by betting on gas. So if you are looking to invest in hedge funds, do your homework and buyer beware!

What is Your "Edge"?

Yes, the market has changed tremendously over the past decade. We are truly no longer in Kansas anymore. So how can a retail investor hope to compete? Believe it or not, a retail investor has some significant edges.

An "edge" is an advantage you have over others. The market for the most part is a zero sum game. If you buy a stock hoping it will rise in price, there is another trader on the other side, selling you the stock and hoping it will go down. You both cannot be right.

What are some of the edges enjoyed by the "little guy" managing his own portfolio? Here are a few.

Activity does not move market
You can instantly buy or sell positions ranging from 100 to several thousand shares without moving the market. Conversely, institutional traders, who may be selling hundreds of thousands of shares, must be careful to space their buy and sell orders over time. Otherwise, their order may move the market to reduce their profits. Some institutions even use algorithms to disguise their activity to make the market believe the orders came from small traders. Thus, you have the advantage of being fast and nimble. Remember the Revolutionary War. The rag-tag Continental Army engaged in guerrilla warfare against the much more powerful and better equipped Redcoats and in the end was victorious. By employing hit and run tactics, you gain an important edge over the "suits" on Wall Street.

Ability to go to cash
You are able to go to cash if you decide the trading environment has become too risky. Mutual Funds and other money managers are prevented from going to cash because of their charter (they are set up to be close to 100% invested at all times). Even if a Large Cap Mutual Fund manager had a crystal ball that told him the market was going to decrease 20% tomorrow, he could do nothing except to find stocks that he hoped would hold up better than the general market (a pretty

difficult task if the overall market is declining). "Not losing" is one of the best ways to win. If the market has you worried, there is no crime in raising cash. Remember, you can always buy back in when a new trend blasts off the launching pad.

Independence

You are independent. You are the boss and can select any stock, sector, or trading vehicle that you like. Most mutual funds are constrained to a certain style. For example, a large cap fund cannot hold small cap stocks. If the large cap mutual fund manager believes that small caps will outperform large caps over the next year, he cannot act on his belief because his prospectus says that he will only invest in large caps. Conversely, you are free to select any investment vehicle that you like. As you will see, you can diversify your portfolio in a manner that will enhance your return while at the same time lowering your risk. If it is advantageous, you can also use more nontraditional asset classes that we will discuss in detail later in the book. If you use this independence in a prudent manner, you have an edge over your better heeled opponents.

Choose Niche Markets

You can choose niche markets that are not heavily traded by mutual funds. Closed End Funds (CEFs) are an excellent example of this category. Commodity ETFs are another example. Your edge comes from utilizing tools and markets that are not available to the typical institutional investor. We will spend significant time discussing how to use these niche markets to rack up profits and reduce risk.

Dr. John Dowdee

Part I
Fundamentals of Developing a Higher Return, Lower Risk Portfolio

Chapter 2. Stocks, Bonds, and Mutual Funds

Chapter 3. Exchange Traded Funds and Notes

Chapter 4. Closed End Funds

Chapter 5. Understanding Futures

Chapter 6. Understanding Call Options

Chapter 7. Evaluating Risk versus Reward

Chapter 8. Asset Allocation and Diversification

Important Notice

To fit the requirements of this book, the figures had to be reduced in size and printed in black and white. To view the charts in full size and in color, please go to www.SuperchargeRetirementIncome.com and click on Book Charts or follow the link below

http://superchargeretirementincome.com/02/knowledge-center/supercharge-retirement-income-charts-for-book/

Dr. John Dowdee

Chapter 2
Stocks, Bonds, and Mutual Funds

Asset allocation is the strategy of spreading your investments across different asset classes. Before the advent of more sophisticated ways to purchase assets, this usually meant spreading your assets among stocks and bonds. In the 1980s and 1990s, mutual funds became the rage. Now mutual funds are giving way to Exchange Traded Funds (ETFs) and Closed End Funds (CEFs). However, before you delve into ETFs or CEFs, you need to be well grounded in the characteristics of stocks, bonds and mutual funds. This chapter serves as a tutorial on these financial vehicles. If you are already an experienced investor, you can skim or skip this chapter.

Common Stock

Common stock represents ownership in a corporation. There are two types of corporations, private and public. A private company may issue stock and have stockholders but the stock is not traded on an exchange. The ownership is private and therefore, the company does not have to meet the filing requirements of the Securities and Exchange Commission (SEC). Since the stock of a private company is not traded, it is often difficult to determine the value of the company. In contrast, a public issues stock via an Initial Public Offering (IPO) and the stock trades on one or more exchanges. Public companies must comply with strict SEC guidelines, including the disclosure of financial statements. In this book, the term "stock" will always refer to a public company. The term stock without any additional qualifier is synonymous with "common stock" and "equity".

A stock represents an ownership share of a public company. Theoretically, this means that a shareholder owns a tiny sliver of all the assets of a company and is entitled to a proportional share of the company earnings. However, it does not mean that you, as a shareholder, have any direct say in the day-to-day management of the company. Instead, each share represents one vote that the shareholder can use to elect a Board of Directors at an annual meeting. The Board of Directors then names the people who will actually manage the company. Hopefully, the management will operate the company in a way that increases the value of the shares you own. However, if the company does not succeed and goes bankrupt, the maximum you can lose is what you paid for the shares. Since companies are organized as corporations, stockholders are not personally liable for any debts incurred by the company.

Why does a company issue stock? Why would the founders of a company decide to share their company with millions of shareholders? The reason is that selling stock is good way to raise money that can then be used to run and expand the business. This is called equity financing and is advantageous since the company does not have to pay back any funds received. In return for providing financing, the stockholder receives a proportional ownership of the company. However, there is no guarantee of how much the stock will be worth in the future.

Dividends

As a company earns money, the Board of Directors may decide to return part of the earnings to the shareholders. This is called a dividend and is typically quoted as a dollar amount per share or as a percentage of the price. The payment and amount of a dividend are not mandatory and are set by the Board of Directors. Some companies, especially high growth companies, plow back all their earnings into the company's operation and do not pay any dividend.

Important dates associated with dividends are:

Declaration Date. This is the date the Board decides to pay a dividend. On this date, the dividend is carried as a liability on the company's books. The board also announces when the dividend will be paid.

Ex-dividend date. This is the date where the owner of record receives the right to receive the dividend. If a person sells his stock after the ex-dividend date, he will still receive the dividend. Since paying the dividend represents a decrease in the company's assets, the stock will typically go down by the amount of the dividend (if all else stays the same).

Payment date. This is the date that the dividend is actually paid. It takes a while to prepare the paperwork associated with paying the dividend so the payment date is a few days after the ex-dividend date.

Brokerage Account

In order to buy or sell a stock, you will require the services of a licensed stock broker. You deposit funds with the broker and he then executes your directives for buying or selling securities (stocks, bonds, mutual funds, etc.). The broker will charge you a fee for each transaction. The broker may even agree to lend you money to allow you to buy more securities than you have funds deposited. This is called a margin account and if you buy securities using borrowed money, this is called "buying on margin", which is a form of leverage. Leverage magnifies gains if you make good decisions but also increases losses if your investments decline. If your total loans relative to your total account size falls below a threshold, the broker will require that you add more cash. This is called a margin call. If you are unable to add cash, the broker has the right to sell some of your holdings to bring your account into compliance with the broker's margin requirements.

In addition to standard and margin accounts, you may also be able to open a retirement account, also called an Individual Retirement Account (IRA) or a 401K account, where gains are not taxed until funds are withdrawn. Another special account can be set up to fund educational expenses. This is called a 529 plan and allows you to save for funding educational with special tax benefits. Each type of account has a set of rules and regulations that you must abide by.

Brokerage accounts come in two flavors: full service and discount. In a full service account, the broker may offer extensive investment advice but will also charge higher fees. A discount broker offers low fees but does not provide any individual buy or sell advice. Most brokerage accounts can be accessed online and buy and sell decisions can be executed in seconds via the internet.

Dr. John Dowdee

The first discount brokerage service was launched by Charles Schwab in 1975. There are now many brokerage firms s including E-Trade, Fidelity, Scottrade, and TD Ameritrade. All brokerages have pluses and minuses so the "best" depends on your particular needs.

Type of Orders
There are many ways you can direct your broker to buy or sell stocks for you. Some of the more popular types of orders are discussed below.

Market Order. This directs your broker to buy or sell a security at the best available price at the time of the order. In a volatile market, this price could change substantially over the course of a day.

Limit Order. This directs your broker to buy or sell a security at a specific price or better. If you sell a stock with a limit order, you are guaranteed to receive your limit price or better (if the broker can find a buyer at the limit price). However, there is no guarantee that your order will be executed. For example, if you direct your broker to sell a stock at a limit price of $10 or better and the stock drops below $10 before your order is executed, you will not be able to sell the stock until you either change the limit price or the stock price recovers (which could potentially be a long time to wait).

Stop Order. A stop order becomes a market order when (and only when) the stock price touches the stop price. Many people use stop orders to try to limit losses that might occur in a stock position. For example, assume you buy Microsoft (MSFT) at $40 per share and set a stop loss order at $36 a share. If the share price drops to $36, then the stock will be sold with a market order. However, you need to be aware that you may not always receive the stop price if the stock gaps lower. For example, assume that MSFT closes on Monday at $36.01 but opens up on Tuesday at $35. The stop order turns into a market order that will sell your security at the best price at the time of the order. In the above example, the best price may be $35, so MSFT will be sold at $35 rather than at the stop price.

Stop Limit Order. This is like a stop order but your stock will only be sold at the limit price or better. This guarantees that you will receive at least the limit price but does not guarantee that the order will be executed.

22

Stock Exchanges

A stock exchange is a place where stock brokers can trade stocks, bonds, and other securities. Each exchange has its own rules for accepting stocks. There are many stock exchanges around the world but the two most prominent stock exchanges are:

New York Stock Exchange (NYSE). This exchange is located at 11 Wall Street and is the world's largest stock exchange. This exchange can trace its history back to 1792 when twenty-four stock brokers met under a buttonwood tree at 68 Wall Street and established rules for buying and selling stocks. This exchange thrived and became one of the most recognized financial institutions in the world. The NYSE was a member's-only club until 2006 when it went public and began to use electronic trading. In 2007, the NYSE merged with the Euronext exchange and in 2013 the NYSE Euronext was acquired by Intercontinental Exchange (ICE). The old American Stock Exchange (AMEX) is also part of this group. Even though it is owned by ICE, the exchange is still called the NYSE.

National Association of Securities Dealers Automated Quotations (NASDAQ). This exchange was founded in 1971 as the world's first electronic stock exchange. NASDAQ was also the first exchange to institute online trading and in 2000, it became a publicly traded company. In 2007, the NASDAQ bought the Philadelphia Stock Exchange, which was the oldest stock exchange in the United States, having been established in 1790. The NASDAQ is the world's second largest stock exchange.

Ticker Symbols

A Ticker Symbol is an alphabetic name that uniquely identifies a stock. Stocks that trade on the New York Stock Exchange (NYSE) have three symbols or less. For example, "T" is the symbol for AT&T, "VZ" is the ticker for Verizon Communications, and "XOM" is the symbol for Exxon Mobile. A stock that trade on the NASDAQ has four or five symbols. For example, "AAPL" is the ticker for Apple and "MSFT" is the symbol for Microsoft. Mutual funds typically have

5 characters in the ticker. For example, "PRRIX" is symbol for PIMCO Real Return mutual fund.

Stocks that do not qualify to trade on a major exchange may be bought and sold via the Over the Counter (OTC) Bulletin Board market or the competing Pink Sheet OTC market. These over the counter markets are used to trade micro-cap companies or penny stocks. The requirements for the OTC market are substantially relaxed in terms of regulation and reporting. The ticker symbols for these stocks typically have 5 letter followed by either an ".OB" (for the Bulletin Board market) or ".PK" for the Pink Sheet market. For example, "TYHJF" is the symbol for Tyhee Gold Corporation, a small mining company that currently sells for about $0.08 a share. Most brokerages can also access these OTC markets but it goes without saying that care should be exercised when buying or selling these off the beaten track stocks. I would also always use limit orders instead of market orders to ensure that you do not receive an unwanted surprise when your order is filled.

Stock Metrics

When considering the purchase of a stock, some of the most important metrics are described below. Most of these metrics can be found online at websites such as: https://finance.yahoo.com/ and http://www.finviz.com.

Price-to-Earnings (P/E) Ratio. This metric is computed by dividing the current price by the annual earnings per share. Historically, the P/E for the entire stock market is about 15 but can vary widely depending on economic conditions. The P/E ratios are also different among industry groups.

The average P/E for different industries can be found at the Yahoo website (http://biz.yahoo.com/p/industries.html).

Price-to-Book (P/B) Ratio. This metric is calculated by dividing the current price by a company's tangible net assets. The P/B changes over time but the current average for the S&P 500 is 2.7. If a stock has a P/B less than 1.5, it is usually considered a "value" stock (unless the low P/B is caused by severe operational problems within the company).

Debt to Equity ratio. This metric is a measure of the how much debt a company has incurred in relation to the company's assets. It is computed as the total liabilities divided by shareholder equity. A high ratio may indicate that a company is using debt to pay bills or expand. The appropriate size of this ratio is heavily dependent on industry. For example, capital intensive industries like utilities may have ratios above 1 while other industries, like technology, could have ratios below 0.5.

P/E ratio to Earnings Growth (PEG). This metric compares the P/E ratio of a company to how fast earnings are growing. The idea is that companies that are rapidly growing earnings should be rewarded with a higher P/E ratio. A low PEG (below 1) might indicate that a stock is undervalued.

Free Cash Flow. A company's earnings are not necessarily the amount of net cash it has received since the calculation of earnings can include accounting items such as depreciations. Free cash flow is a better metric than earnings to assess how much cash a company has for paying dividends or expansion. Free cash flow is the amount of cash on hand after capital expenditures.

Bonds

Bonds are debt instruments (like a formal IOU). The investor loans money to an entity (a company or the government) and the loan is repaid over a fixed period of time at a fixed rate of interest. Bonds are called "fixed income" because the repayment of the loan is fixed by the bond contract and does not change over time.

Types of Bonds
Bonds come in different flavors depending on who borrows the money. The most common types are listed below.

Government Bonds (Treasuries). Government bonds are classified as "Treasuries" and can be further portioned according to their time to maturity as follows

1) Bills. Debts that will mature in less than a year

2) Notes. Debts that will mature in one to ten years.

3) Bonds. Debts that will mature in more than ten years.

Agency-backed Bonds (Agencies). Agency-backed bonds are bonds issued by Government Sponsored Agencies (GSEs). These are bonds that have the implicit backing of the U.S Government (but not explicitly like treasuries).

Municipal Bonds. Municipal bonds (also called munis) are bonds insured by municipalities, either cities or states. The advantage of munis is that they are exempt from federal tax. In some cases, they may also be exempt from state taxes. Because of the lesser tax benefits, muni's typically have lower yield than other types of bonds of similar credit quality.

Corporate Bonds. Companies issue bonds to raise money. The interest rate on corporate bonds depends on the credit worthiness of the corporation but is generally higher than risk-free government bonds. A convertible corporate bond is one that has an added feature of being convertible into common stock under some predefined conditions.

Foreign bonds. Foreign bonds are those issued by foreign governments or corporations. Why invest in these international bonds? Typically there are two reasons:

1) Diversification. Foreign bonds rise and fall due to local conditions which may not be in sync with the U.S. market, thus offering diversification to a fixed income portfolio.

2) Higher returns. Since the risks are usually higher, the yields are also higher. This is true especially for emerging markets where political instability, lack of infrastructure, and the currency volatility exacerbate the risks.

Foreign bonds may trade in either the currency associated with their country of origin or trade in U.S. dollars. The bonds that trade in local currency have an additional risk due to the fluctuations in foreign exchange rates

Bond terms
Maturity. The date that the bond can be redeemed for the face value is called the maturity date of the bond. Until the maturity date, bonds pay interest at intervals set forth in the bond document.

Coupon. The coupon is another word for interest rate. In the previous non-electronic age, bond holders were issued a certificate with coupons attached. At appropriate times, the bond owner would tear off the coupon and present it for payment.

Zero Coupon Bond. A bond where all the coupons have been removed so there are no interest payments. The bond can still be redeemed on the maturity date for the face value. Because a zero-coupon bond does not pay interest, it sells at a discount to allow the buyer to make a profit when he eventually redeems the bond.

Par. Another name for the face value of the bond is "par". Depending on conditions, if you sell a bond before the maturity date, the price may be above or below par. For example, assume you have a $1,000 bond with one year before maturity. The bond has a coupon rate of 5% so the bond buyer will receive $50 in interest over the next year. However, suppose the current interest rate is 10% so you could buy a newly issued bond and receive $100 per year interest. Therefore, if you want to sell your bond before maturity, you will need to assure the buyer that if he buys your bond he will still receive $100 interest. You can do this by discounting the price of your bond to $950. The buyer would then receive $50 in interest and $50 in gains when the bond matures so buying your bond is equivalent to investing in newly issued bond. This illustrates why some bonds sell below par. The reverse is also true. If the current interest rate is only 1%, then a bond that pays 5% interest will be worth more than par.

Yield. This is the actual annual rate of return you expect to receive by buying the bond. It is equal to the coupon rate only if the bond is selling at par. The actual rate of return you receive depends on the coupon rate in relation to the price you paid for the bond.

Duration. Duration is a complex financial metric that measures the sensitivity of the bond price to changes in interest rates. The larger the duration, the greater the bond price will decrease if interest rates rise (or similarly, the bond price will rise if interest rates fall)

Callability. If a bond is callable, the issuing company has the right to redeem the bond before maturity. The conditions under which the bond can be called are described in the bond agreement. A company may decide to redeem a bond if interest rates are falling and the company can obtain a better deal by issuing new debt.

Secured bonds. These are loans that are secured by some collateral. A car loan is an example of a loan secured by the automobile that you are buying. Another example is a home loan that is secured by your house. This collateral provides additional security in case the company goes bankrupt.

Mortgage-backed security. This is a bond secured by one or more mortgages.

Non-secured bonds. These bonds are also called debentures and are not backed by collateral.

Default. Default occurs when the issuing company fails to make an interest payment or cannot redeem the bond at maturity. Default is an extremely serious situation and could cause the company to file for bankruptcy. In the event of a bankruptcy, secured bonds holders are paid first and then unsecured bond holders. Stockholders are paid last.

Bond Ratings

An independent agency such as Standard and Poor's, Moody's, or Fitch analyze bonds in terms of the ability for the issuer to actually pay the interest and principal associated with the bond. The nomenclature of the ratings depends on the particular rating agency with Standard and Poor's and Fitch employing the same symbols and Moody's having a slightly different system. The Standard and Poor's/Fitch rate bonds as follows (with pluses and minuses used to differentiate subtle differences within a category.

AAA and AA: Highest credit quality

AA and BBB: Medium credit quality

BB, B, CCC, CC, C: Low credit quality

D: Bonds that are already in default.

Moody's uses a similar rating system but the nomenclature uses both capital and lower case levels plus numbers rather than pluses and minuses. For example, a Standard and Poor's AA+ is equivalent to a Moody's Aa1. A complete description of ratings can be found on Wikipedia at http://en.wikipedia.org/wiki/Bond_credit_rating.

The first two categories BBB to AAA are called "investment grade". The lower ratings are termed non-investment grade. These low rated bonds are also called "junk bonds".

Interest Rates

The major determinants of the amount of interest rate a company must pay to borrow money are credit quality and duration.

The higher the credit quality of a company, the lower the interest since the risk of default is small. The ultimate credit quality is the United States Government so Treasury bonds usually have lower rates than corporate bonds. Non-investment grade bonds are called "High Yield" since these bonds must pay higher interest rates (also referred to as the yield) in order to attract buyers.

Maturity is the other major driver of the amount of interest rate. The plot of the level of the yield as a function of time to maturity is called the "yield curve". The yield curve normally slopes upward, meaning that the longer the maturity, the higher the interest rate that must be paid. However, in some anomalous economic conditions, the yield curve may be inverted so that interest rates are higher for shorter maturities. This usually means that investors are expecting a recession that would drive future interest rates lower.

Preferred Stock

Many companies issue preferred stock in addition to their common shares. This is one way corporations can raise money without diluting the number of common shares. Preferred stock does not have voting rights but usually has a much higher dividend than the common stock. The dividend payment associated with preferred stock is not guaranteed but the preferred stockholder must be paid before the common stockholder can receive any dividends. Thus, preferred stock sits between bonds and common stock in the capital structure. It is senior to the common stock but will be paid after the interest on bonds. Suspending payments on preferred stock is a last resort but it is not considered a default like suspending payment to bondholders.

Preferred stocks are issued in fixed denominations (for example, $25 per share or $50 per share are typical amounts). The shares are traded on the open market so the price may fluctuate after the stock is issued. The fluctuations are usually less than the common stock.

But beware if the company gets into trouble and investors believe the dividend may be suspended. In this case, the price can fall dramatically. This happened in 2008 when some preferred stocks that were issued at $25 per share were selling for significantly below $20 per share. If the company (and the preferred) subsequently recovers, you could make a nice capital gain in addition to collecting the dividends. However, this is the exception rather than the rule. Under normal conditions, people buy preferred stock for income, not capital gains.

Data on Preferred Stock

It is much more difficult to obtain data on preferred stocks than their common counterparts. The best source for data is http://www.quantumonline.com/. By typing in the common stock name, for example BAC for Bank of America, you will be taken to a Bank of America page. Click on "Find All Related Securities for BAC" and this will list all the preferred stocks that have been issued. For BAC, this is a long list. The symbols that are bolded are active (many of the issues may be obsolete and no longer trading).

The symbol for preferred stocks is usually the common symbol plus a letter. For example, BAC-J is the "Bank of America, 7.25% Dep Shares Non-Cumulative Preferred Stock, Series J". If you click on this Series J link, you are taken to another page that describes the preferred in detail. It provides the coupon rate, the offering price, call date (if any), call price, the Moody's rating, and the distribution dates.

Preferred stocks are either perpetual (without any maturity date) or have long maturities that could be more than 30 years. However, some preferred stocks, like bonds, are "callable" at some time in the future for a designated amount (usually the issue price). For example, the call date for this BAC Series J is 11/01/12. This call date is in the past, which means that BAC can call the preferred (that is, purchase the stock from you) at any time, at BAC's discretion. If they decide to call in the preferred, you do not have a choice—you have to sell it at the indicated call price.

Note also that this preferred is "non-cumulative". If a preferred is "cumulative" this means that if the company misses a dividend payment but then resumes dividend payments in the future, then the preferred stockholder must be paid all the missed dividends. This is an excellent provision but unfortunately only a few preferred stocks are cumulative. As the name implies, if the preferred stock is "non-cumulative", then the company does not have to repay missed dividends. Cumulative preferred are more valuable than non-cumulative and usually trade at higher price, if all other parameters are equal.

How to buy preferred stock

Preferred stocks can be easily traded in your brokerage account but first you must find the symbol, which may not be as easy as it sounds. Each broker has their own way of naming preferred stock. For example, for Schwab, preferred stocks are denoted by a "/PR" after the symbol. For example, the Series J BAC preferred we looked at above has the symbol BAC/PRJ at Schwab. As of 4/4/14, this market price of this preferred is 25.50. So it is selling a little more than its issue price which reduces the yield from 7.25% (at issue) to about 7%. You would not expect this preferred to appreciate too much more since it can be called at any time by Bank of America for $25.00

Mutual Funds

Mutual funds are a type of professionally managed investment vehicle that pools money from many individuals to buy assets. The types of assets that the fund manager can purchase are restricted by the charter of the fund, which you can read in fund's Prospectus. Funds may invest in stocks or bonds (or other assets as long as they are disclosed in the Prospectus). Funds are regulated and are sold to the general public. If there is no fee to purchase the fund, they are called "no load" funds. If a fee is charged, they are called "load" funds. A reasonable investment strategy is to purchase only no-load funds since performance appears to be independent of whether or not a load is charged.

Funds can be bought or sold only at the end of each day and the price is equal to the Net Asset Value (NAV). NAV is the value (as determined by market price at the end of the day) of all the assets in the fund.

Mutual funds can be actively managed (where the manager decides which stocks or bonds to buy) or it can be an Index Fund (where the fund tries to match the performance of an index, such as the S&P 500).

Open End Funds

There are two types of funds: open end funds and closed end funds. The term mutual fund refers to open end funds. Closed end funds are very different from open end funds and will be discussed in Chapter 4.

A mutual fund is also called an "open end fund" since it does not have any restrictions on the number of shares the fund will issue. At the end of the day, the open end funds buys back shares at the NAV from investors that wish to sell. If there are more buyers than sellers, the fund then issues more shares so that demand always equals supply. Therefore, open end funds sell at the NAV (calculated at the end of each day after the market is closed); there is never any discount or premium. As we will see later, closed end funds may sell at significant discounts or premiums. Note that when a mutual fund manager determines that the total assets are becoming too large to manage, he can close the fund to new investors. Even though the names are similar, a closed mutual fund is completely different from a closed end fund.

The idea of an open end fund goes back to 1907 when the Alexander Fund had many attributes of the modern mutual fund. Mutual funds have become extremely popular and by the end of 2012, the number of funds had mushroomed to over 7,000. However, in recent years the draw of mutual funds has diminished and has been replaced by the new kid on the block, Exchange Traded Funds. Exchange Traded Funds will be discussed in Chapter 3.

Bond Mutual funds

As the name implies, bond funds are just mutual funds that invest in bonds rather than stocks. The main difference between purchasing a bond fund rather than a bond is that the bond is guaranteed to pay you the face amount at maturity (unless the issuing company goes bankrupt). A bond fund does not have a maturity date and you are not guaranteed to recover your principal if the fund goes down in price (which can happen if interest rates rise). On the plus side, bond funds are easier to buy and sell and have a built-in diversification that is difficult to obtain by purchasing individual bonds.

Government Regulation

Before leaving this exposition on funds, it will be worthwhile to briefly review the history of government regulation. In 1928, after the go-go years of the roaring twenties, there were 19 open end funds and more than 700 closed end funds and virtually no government oversight of their activities. After the market crash of 1929 and the ensuing Great Depression, many of the highly-levered closed end funds were wiped out and the government started to take an interest. The Securities and Exchange Commission (SEC) was created in 1934 to regulate commerce in bonds, stocks, and funds. Mutual funds were required to register with the SEC and to provide disclosure statements called a "prospectus" to potential investors. The next major improvement was the Investment Company Act of 1940, which clearly defined the responsibilities and limitations placed on funds. This objective of this act was to protect the interests of the investing public and to instill confidence that the funds would deliver on their promises. The act provided guidelines on the valuation of funds' assets, restrictions on conflicts of interest, and limits on the amount of leverage that could be utilized. This act has been refined over the years, with the latest update being the Dodd Frank Act of 2010.

Dr. John Dowdee

Chapter 3
Exchange Traded Funds (ETFs)

Over the last couple of decades, an alternative to traditional mutual funds has emerged and has revolutionized the investment landscape. This innovation was called an Exchange Traded Fund (ETF). An ETF is a basket of securities that are traded on an exchange just like individual stocks. For example, you can buy ETFs that contain all the constituents of the S&P 500 or and ETF that contains all the components of the Russell 2000. Thus ETFs give the investor unprecedented ability to easily construct a diversified portfolio with only a few purchases.

Like all investments, there are advantages and disadvantages of investing in ETFs. This chapter will provide the insights you will need to determine whether ETFs are right for you.

Diversification

One of the reasons that mutual funds became popular is that they allowed an easy way for an individual investor to own a basket of stocks. However, one of the problems with mutual funds is that they can only be bought and sold at the end of the day. This is usually not a problem but what if the market is moving fast during the day. You may not want to wait until the close to buy and sell. The development of Exchange Traded Funds in the early 1990s solved this problem by offering the investor the best of both worlds--a basket of stocks that are bundled together and can be traded throughout the day, just like an individual stock. As the name suggests, ETF are funds (that is baskets of stocks) that can be traded on an exchange during the day.

ETFs are extremely popular. There are roughly 1,400 ETFs covering just about any asset class or combination of asset classes that an investor might desire. Using ETFs you can construct a portfolio that meets a wide range of investment objectives, from conservative to aggressive and from conventional to nontraditional.

How ETFs are created

ETFs can only be created by large financial institutions that meet regulatory requirements plus have the "deep pockets" to put an ETF together. You do not need to know how ETFs are created to trade them. However, it is useful to know the background so that you can understand some of the unique characteristics of ETFs.

First, the company that wants to launch an ETF files a plan with the Securities Exchange Commission (SEC). Once the plan is approved, authorized participants can begin to buy the ETFs in huge chunks called creation units. A creation unit is typically tens to hundreds of thousands of share of the ETF. These creations units are held by custodial banks who buy the equivalent assets represented by the ETF. Thus, the assets associated with the ETF are held in "escrow" so that the ETF cannot be devalued by some anomaly not associated with the underlying assets. This is an important consideration for ETFs; in most cases they actually hold the basket of assets that they are representing.

The authorized participant now holds thousands of shares of an ETF and can trade them on the open market. If they want to "cash out", they would have to buy sufficient shares that make up their creation unit and turn the creation unit back to the custodial bank and receive the underlying assets that can then be sold on the open market. Because the ETF is freely exchangeable for the underlying assets, the price of the ETF does not stray far from the value of the underlying assets, called the Net Asset Value (NAV). For example, if due to market pressures, the price of the ETF becomes substantially more than the price of its constituent parts, an authorized participant can create more units of the ETF and sell them to the market. The additional supply will then drive the price of the ETF down to be approximately equal to the NAV.

Thus, it is rare for the shares of an ETF to deviate substantially from the NAV. However, as discussed in the "Tracking Error" section below, under some circumstance there may be some deviation. As we will see in the next chapter, this characteristic is completely different for Closed End Funds (where it is common for funds to trade at substantial premiums and discounts).

Comparison with Mutual Funds

ETFs are better than index mutual funds in several ways. ETFs are more flexible since they can be traded during the day. You can also use any type of order to buy an ETF, such as market, limit, and stop orders. In addition, you can buy ETFs on margin and can even sell them short. Since an ETF usually trades a passive index, the cost of operating an ETF is typically (but not always) less than you would expect from a similar mutual fund.

On the negative side, a disadvantage of an ETF occurs if you trade it often. For every trade, you must pay the broker a commission so if you are an active trader, you may end up paying more for the ETF than you would have paid for an equivalent mutual fund. However, even though you may be able to buy and sell mutual funds for no costs, many mutual funds limit the number of buy and sell transaction allowed by the fund over a specified period.

Another disadvantage for some ETFs may be liquidity. Since ETFs trade like stocks, they are subject to the buy-sell spreads from the market makers. If an ETF is thinly traded, the buy-sell spread could be large, increasing the costs of trading. If the ETF trades less than 50,000 shares per day, you should always use limit orders when buying and selling.

ETFs may also be more tax efficient than mutual funds. In a mutual fund, the manager may have to sell some of the holdings to raise cash for redemptions. These redemptions may result in capital gains, which are passed on to the investor as taxable events at the end of the year. In contrast, trading in ETFs is done between shareholders on the open market (just like any other stock) so ETF managers do not have to sell holding to make redemptions. However the ETF may have to buy and sell assets if the index it is tracking changes. These tracking adjustments may also result in taxable capital gain events.

Tracking Error

An ETF is a security that tracks an index. The ETF can achieve this tracking by purchasing a basket of assets (usually stocks or bonds but future contracts and options can also be used). The popularity of ETFs stems from the many varied indexes that are available. You can trade virtually any type of asset using ETFs. Want to trade stocks from Singapore? No problem. There are indexes constructed to track stocks domiciled in Singapore. How about trading gold? No problem, you do not have to purchase gold bars or coins. There are indexes that track the price of gold bullion. The only limit to the variety of ETF is the imagination of the ETF originator (and of course the acceptance of the product by investors).

The tracking error associated with an ETF is the difference between the return from ETF and the return from the underlying index. In other words, tracking error is a measure of how well the ETF tracks the associated index. If the ETF holds all the assets within the index, then the tracking error is small. For example, the SPDR S&P 500 (SPY) ETF holds all 500 stocks in the same proportion as the index. Thus, SPY tracks the index almost perfectly, with the only difference being the fee charged by the ETF, which reduces the return.

However, some ETFs are based on indexes that are not that easy to duplicate. For example, the MSCI Emerging Market Index tracks 765 stocks in 24 different countries, many of which trade in different currencies. As you can image, an ETF based on this index would be hard to replicate exactly.

To solve this problem, ETTs may use a technique called representative sampling by buying a smaller number of stocks that they hope will mirror the performance of the underlying index. Sometime this works but sometimes this creates relatively large tracking errors, especially when the market is becomes highly volatile like in 2000 and 2008.

The average tracking error of all ETFs is about 0.6%, which is not bad. But the numbers can vary widely by asset class and the liquidity of the underlying components. For example, commodity, emerging market, and currency ETFs typically have larger tracking errors than run of the mill equity ETFs. Some of the more extreme examples of tracking errors are summarized below.

- iShares FTSE NAREIT Mortgage REIT ETF (REM) underperformed the index by almost 12% in 2008
- Vanguard Telecommunications Services ETF (VOX) underperformed the index by about 6% in 2008
- United Natural Gas ETF (UNG) sold at a premium of 20% in 2009 because the creation of new units was suspended until the Authorized Participants received clarification of some regulatory issues

Thus, ETFs do not always follow their underlying index exactly due to rules, regulations, and other shortcomings. It is important that you understand potential tracking errors when you invest in ETFs.

Exchange Traded Notes (ETNs)

ETNs are cousins to ETFs and serve basically the same purpose for traders. ETNs also track indexes but there are some indexes where it is difficult to actually buy the basket of assets. For example, suppose you want to track the price of sugar. It would be difficult and expensive to buy sugar and keep it in a warehouse. So ETNs were invented.

ETNs are structured products that are issued by major banks as senior debt notes. The return you receive from the note is structured to give you the same return you would receive if you could purchase a particular index. The main difference between an ETF and an ETN is that the ETN is debt product whereas the ETF actually owns the underlying assets. Since ETNs are backed by banks with high credit rating, they usually do not have significant credit risk. ETNs usually track indexes related to currencies, commodities, some energy products, and to strategy indexes such as the Buy/Write.

One advantage of ETNs is the lack of tracking error. The ETNs are notes where the holder is promised a contractual rate of return tied to the underlying index. So the issuing bank is obligated to pay the holder the same return (less fees) as would be obtained by investing in the underlying index.

In practice, ETFs and ETNs are very similar to one another and the term ETF is often used to refer to ETNs. A more precise description is to use the term Exchange Traded Products (ETPs) to refer to both types of exchange traded vehicles. In this book, the term ETF will also mean ETNs unless there is a particular reason to be more precise.

ETF Stock Classifications

Investors usually categorize stocks by putting then in different buckets like the ones described below. ETFs use these classifications to describe the index they are tracking.

Market Capitalization
Market Capitalization of a company is the total dollar value of the company's outstanding stock. It can be computed as the price of the stock times the total number of available shares of the stock. There is no set rule for defining the different categories but generally:

Large Cap is a company valued at more than $10 billion

Mid Cap is a company valued between $1 billion and $10 billion

Small Cap is a company valued at between $300 million and $1 billion

Micro-Cap is a company less than $300 million

Weighting
An index is composed of the number of companies but the index developer does not have to treat each component equally; some might be given more emphasis than others. For example, think about how tiles are valued in the game of Scrabble. The letter Z is worth 10 points while an E is worth only 1 point. Thus, when you play a word, the value you receive depend on the value or "weight" assigned to each letter. The same principle can be applied to indexes.

Indexes are computed using a weighted average based on some parameter, such as the market capitalization of the underlying securities. A weighted average is obtained by multiplying the price of each component by the weight. Note that mathematically the values of all the weights must sum to one.

Let's look at an example. Suppose you want to construct an index based on the price of two stocks, A and B. Assume each stock is selling for $10 a share. An equal weight index would have two weights that are equal. Since the weights sum to one, each weight is 0.5. The value of this Equal Weight Index can be computed as:

Equal Weight Index = 0.5*10 +0.5*10 = 10

Now assume the price of stock A increases by $1 to 11 and the price of stock B decreases by $1 to 9. The index is now computed as

Equal Weight Index = 0.5*11 + 0.5*9 = 5.5 + 4.5 = 10.

So the index does not change since the weights are equal and the fluctuations cancel each other.

Now assume that we construct a non-equal weight by assigning the price of stock A a weight of 0.75 and stock B a weight of 0.25. Now if the price of A increases by $1 and the price of B decreases by $1, the value of the Weighted Index is computed as:

Weighted Index = (.75*11 +.25*9) = 8.25 + 2.25 = 10.5

In this case, the value of the Weighted Index is higher than the Equal Weight Index because Stock A was given more weight.

Based on the above example, it should be easier to understand some to the more common ways to weight an index.

Cap weighted. As we have discussed, market cap is the total value of the company. Many indexes are cap weighted so that larger companies have more weight than smaller companies. For example, in the S&P 500, the smallest company is Meredith Corporation (MDH). Thus to compute value of the S&P 500, you multiply the price of MDH by its weight of 0.000114. Compare this to Exxon Mobile (XOM), the largest company in the S&P 500. To compute the value S&P 500, the price of XOM is weighted by .031172. Thus XOM has 272 times more impact on the S&P 500 than MDH.

The majority of indexes are cap weighted since it is intuitive that what happens to a large company should have more impact than perturbations in a small company. However, some people do not care about size and want to achieve diversification by spreading risk equally over companies, regardless of size. This gave rise to the Equal Weight Indexes.

Equal Weight. Some ETFs are based on an equal weight index. Each component in the index is treated the same. This means the contributions from a small company is the same as a large company. An example of equal weighting is the S&P Equal Weight Index which uses .002 for the weight of each component (note the weights sum to one since .002*500 =1).

Price Weighted. In this index scheme, the influence is proportional to the price per share. The Dow Jones Industrial Average uses price weighting. Except for the DOW, this type of weighting is seldom used since it gives more weight to higher priced stocks, regardless of how many shares are outstanding. If a stock splits, it will have less weight in the index.

Fundamental Weighted. This is a recent development in the creation of indexes where the weights are determined by some fundamental factor such as earning, book value, or dividend yield.

Style
Many portfolio managers follow one of two investment styles: growth or value. Growth managers look for companies with above average growth profiles, usually companies that have a unique niche that is growing. On the other hand, value managers look for inexpensive stocks that they believe are undervalued by some metric. The exact demarcation between these styles is not cast in concrete and different index providers use different metrics. For example, the Russell 1000 Value Index selects stocks based on lower price-to-book. In contrast, the Russell 1000 Growth Index selects stocks based on higher price-to-book coupled with higher forecasted earnings growth. When an index contains both value and growth stocks, like the S&P 500, it is typically called a blend. You can buy ETFs that only have growth stocks, or value stocks, or a blend. This allows you to tailor your ETF portfolio to your investment objectives.

Sectors
Stocks can also be partitioned into Sectors, where a sector is defined as a group of companies that have similar behaviors, laws, and

regulations. As an example, Standard and Poor's partitions stocks into the following 9 sectors.

Consumer Discretionary. This sector comprises companies that sell non-essential goods and services. Some examples are retail stores, media firms, automotive companies, hotels, restaurants, leisure equipment, apparel, and luxury goods. This sector does well when the economy is strong and consumers have extra money to spend on non-essential items.

Consumer Staples. This sector consists of companies that sell essential products such as food, beverages, household items, and tobacco. The products of these companies are always in demand, regardless of economic conditions. Companies within this sector often have slow but steady growth.

Energy. This sector consists of integrated oil companies as well as companies that specialize in exploration, oil services, and drilling. The performance of the sector is based on supply and demand and as you would expect, companies do well when oil and gas prices are high. This sector is also sensitive to political events, especially those that might disrupt the flow of oil.

Financial. This sector consists of commercial banks, brokerage houses, insurance companies, consumer finance firms, and Real Estate Investment Trusts (REITs). The financial sector performs best in a low interest rate environment and when the economy is on the upswing. As the economy improves, businesses make more investments and consumers spend more, which bodes well for the financial sector.

Healthcare. This sector consists of companies that provide healthcare and medical services. This sector is typically considered defensive since healthcare is not discretionary. Having a steady demand for goods makes this sector less sensitive to the economic cycle.

Industrial. This sector consists of companies providing goods used in construction and manufacturing. This sector includes aerospace and defense, construction companies, machinery companies, transportation firms, and industrial conglomerates. The sector does best when the economy is booming and companies are expanding.

Materials. This sector is comprised of companies that are involved the discovery, development, and processing of raw materials. This sector includes chemical, mining, paper, forestry products, and construction material companies. This sector is sensitive to the economic cycle. If the economy is strong, the demand for more raw materials typically increases.

Technology. Technology companies are involved in the development or distribution of technology products such as computers, electronics, software, and information systems. Technology is a fast evolving sector and offers products to the Government, businesses, and the consumer. Technology fads tend to come and go with breath-taking advances followed by equally impressive drops.

Utilities. The utility sector consists of large firms that operate facilities for the generation and transmission of electricity, gas, or water to the general public. These firms usually require substantial infrastructure, like power distribution lines, and they have to assume large amounts of debt to finance expansion and improvements. This makes utility companies sensitive to interest rates. However, once the infrastructure is in place, it becomes cost prohibitive for other companies to compete. Therefore, utilities often enjoy a "natural monopoly" in the region they serve. The Government also views utilities as providing essential services for the well-being of society. For these reasons, many of the utilities companies are regulated. The regulators set retail rates that are designed to provide each company with a "fair" rate of return. This provides a stable income for the regulated companies but decreases their ability to grow profits.

Other ETF Classification
There are many other ways to classify an ETF. Some of the more common classifications are discussed below.

International or Single Countries. ETFs are a great way to invest in a basket of international stocks or stocks from a specific country. You can also choose among developed economies or emerging markets. Virtually every country now has one or more funds devoted to stocks domiciled within their border. Or you can choose regions, like Europe, the Far East, or Latin America. The choices are almost endless.

Fixed Income. Fixed income usually refers to a debt instrument that pays a fixed amount each month. The most common type of fixed income assets are bonds but fixed income could take other forms such as loans. There are hosts of fixed income ETFs that cover one or more of the bond types described below.

Commodities. These are funds that invest in commodities such as agriculture or metals. The ETF can invest in a wide range of commodities or can limit themselves to a specific commodity such as corn, coffee, sugar, gold, or silver. These ETFs usually use futures to provide the required exposure. These futures based ETFs typically have little correlation with stocks and therefore provide portfolio diversification.

Currencies. Currency ETFs are invested in a single currency or a basket of currencies with the objective of replicating the movements in the Foreign Exchange (FOREX) market. These ETFs track the value of currencies relative to one another by either holding these currencies are by using currency denominated short term debt. These ETFs allow an investor to participate in the FOREX market without having to use futures or open a forex account. Some of the more popular currencies being traded are the Canadian and Australian dollars, the Euro, the British Pound, and the Japanese Yen.

Real Estate Investment Trusts (REITs). A REIT ETFs invests in real estate, either through properties or mortgages. These ETFs allow investors to participate in the real estate market without the burden of managing rentals or being limited to specific properties or real estate sectors. The underlying securities are publically traded real estate trusts. These ETFs are a hybrid between equity and fixed income in that they typically have above average dividend yields but can also fluctuate with the equity market.

Alternative Strategies. You can now find ETFs developed around specific strategies. Want to focus on dividend paying stocks? No problem, there are many ETFs devoted to dividend payers. Or maybe you want to invest in only low volatility stocks. Again, no problem. There are now a number of low volatility ETFs. You can also short the market by investing in inverse ETFs (you can even hold these in a retirement account that does not allow direct shorting of stocks). If you can think of a viable strategy, there is likely an ETF that will help you implement it. The choices are truly mind boggling!

Chapter 4
Closed End Funds (CEFs).

Closed End Funds (CEFs) have been around for more than 120 years but are still not widely used or understood by investors. At a basic level, a CEF is a cross between a stock and a mutual fund, with some characteristics of each.

Similar to a mutual fund, a CEF invests in a basket of stocks, bonds, or other investment vehicles. However, like a stock, a CEF comes into existence via an Initial Public Offering (IPO), where a fixed number of shares are sold to the public. The proceeds from the IPO are used by the fund manager to purchase securities. After the IPO, the shares of the CEF are listed on an exchange and traded just like any other stock. You can buy and sell shares of a CEF throughout the day by entering an order with your broker.

Sources of Capital

After the IPO, there are only 5 ways a manager can increase the amount of capital under management.

1) He can make good investment decisions that will increase the value of the securities held.

2) He can incur debt that has to be repaid with interest. This borrowed money gives the manager more capital to invest and if he can achieve a return higher than the interest costs, this will add value to the fund. The use of borrowed money to buy additional securities is called "leverage".

3) He can sell "preferred shares" to the public and invest the proceeds. Preferred stock does not have voting rights but typically has a larger dividend, which must be paid before common shares. Preferred stock is usually viewed as a hybrid that has some attributes of common stock and some similarities to bonds. The dividend on preferred shares is similar to interest payments on debt.

4) He can conduct a secondary offering. This is similar to an IPO in that new shares are sold to the public. However, since it is not the first offering, it is called a secondary offering. Just like the IPO, the secondary offering raises capital but it also increases the number of shares outstanding.

5) The final way to increase the amount of capital is by a "rights offering". This gives existing shareholders the right to invest more capital into the fund by buying more shares at specified prices. This is similar to a secondary offering except it is not open to the general public and only current shareholders can participate.

Note that the amount of capital the manager has to invest is not affected by the selling price of the CEF.

The amount of capital under management can also decrease. This occurs primarily for two reasons:

1) The manager makes poor investment decisions that incur losses.

2) The manger decides to return some of the cash to shareholders. This is called a "distribution" and can come from income received from investments, capital gains received from selling investments at a profit, or Return of Capital (ROC). ROC will be discussed in more detail later in the chapter.

Premiums/Discounts

The total amount of securities in the fund (less any liabilities) divided by the number of outstanding shares is called the Net Asset Value (NAV). However, this is not necessarily the price you will pay for the CEF. The price you pay is based strictly on supply and demand. If the demand is strong, some investors may be willing to pay more than the NAV and the funds is said to sell at a premium. Similarly, if the supply of shares offered for sale exceeds the demand, the fund may sell at a discount to the NAV. The size of the premium or discount will vary from minute to minute as the CEF trades during the day.

Selling at a discount/premium is an important distinction between an open ended mutual fund and a closed end fund. The NAV of a mutual fund is calculated only once per day and that is the price that that buyers pay and sellers receive. Mutual funds do not sell at a discount or premium. To avoid discounts or premiums, the number of outstanding shares of a mutual fund is adjusted at the end of the day, so that supply always equals demand. This can have some unintended consequences. If a significant number of investors decide to sell their mutual fund, then the mutual fund company must buy back all the shares at the end of the day at the NAV. Thus, the mutual funds must either maintain cash for the buybacks or may have to raise cash by selling some of their securities. This sometimes requires managers to sell securities they would rather not sell.

The CEF does not buy back shares at the end of the day. The number of shares stays constant. Thus the CEF manager does not have to worry about selling securities to meet redemption demands. This means that the CEF manager can invest in less liquid securities and he does not have to hold a large amount of cash.

Distribution Rates

Most CEFs are organized as Regulated Investment Companies (RICs) and do not pay taxes. This is an important distinction between a CEF and a corporation. A CEF does not have "double taxation" because it acts like a conduit that passes gains to the investor. Generally, CEFs must pass 90% of income and 98% of realized capital gains to their shareholders. The amount of money distributed is called the "distribution" and is usually expressed as a percentage of the price (or alternatively a percentage of the NAV).

The funds for distributions are derived from 4 sources:

1) Interest payments received from fixed income investments such as bonds

2) Dividends received from equity holdings

3) Realized capital gains from selling a security

4) Return of capital (ROC). ROC happens when the amount of distribution exceeds the cash received from the previous three sources. Return of capital is a relatively complicated subject and is often misunderstood. ROC will be discussed in detail later in the chapter.

Note that distributions should not really be called "yield" because the source usually has capital gains as well as interest payments or dividends. Similarly, distributions should not be called "dividends" since the funds may not all come from money received from equity holdings. The most accurate way to refer to income received from CEFs is to just to call them "distributions".

It is important to know the source of a distribution. Distributions coming from interest payments and dividends are relatively "safe", that is, they can likely be repeated in the future. However, income that is dependent on capital gains is not as stable and should be given less weight. Income from ROC is in a class by itself and will be discussed later. The source of the distribution can usually be obtained from the website maintained by the CEF or from http://www.cefconnect.com.

Leverage

A CEF often has much high distribution rates than can be received from mutual funds or exchange traded funds. One of the reasons is that CEFs can use leverage. Since leverage increases the amount of capital, it can also increase the amount of income generated by the capital. If assets are appreciating more than the interest rates associated with borrowed funds, leverage is generally good. But if the assets are decreasing in value (for example, in a bear market), leverage will exacerbate the decline. Over long periods of time, studies indicate that leverage has more benefits than drawbacks. However, leverage will almost always increase the volatility of a fund.

The amount of leverage that a CEF can utilize is regulated by the Investment Company Act of 1940. A CEF can assume debt up to 50% of its NAV and can issue preferred stock up to 100% of net assets. Usually CEFs limit their leverage to about 33%. For example, if a fund has $1 in assets, it will typically invest a total of $1.33 cents.

Expense Ratio

The expense ratio is an important metric when evaluation CEFs. The expense ratio is reported as a percentage of net assets.

The fund manager tries to increase the value of the CEF by making good investments so that he can reward his investors. To compensate him for efforts, he collects a fee, typically as a percentage of the assets under management, including the assets purchased using leverage. This fee is part of the expense ratio.

Since expenses are reported as a percentage of NAV but management charges are against total assets, the management fees associated with most CEFs are relatively high when compared to mutual funds.

The other part of the expense ratio is the interest paid on debt used for leverage. However, as we have discussed, preferred stock can also be issued to increase leverage. The payments made to preferred stockholders are not included in the expense ratio.

Return of Capital (ROC)

Return of capital is an important concept when investing in Closed End Funds. As discussed, for tax purposes, the cash available for distributions comes only from interest, dividends, and realized capital gains made in the current period. If a fund distributes more than this cash, it is considered return of capital.

However, not all ROC is considered "bad". For example, if fund assets have appreciated but have not been sold, then the NAV has increased by what is called "unrealized capital gains". When it comes time for a distribution, a fund manager may decide not to sell some of his best performing assets because he believes they will appreciate even more. If he had sold the asset, he would have had plenty of cash for the distribution. However, since he decided not to sell, he may have a shortfall and not enough "immediate" cash flow to pay the distribution. He therefore has to delve into savings, which results in a tax event that is termed "return of capital". This type of ROC is not destructive.

Let's look at an example. Suppose a fund has $100 in assets with $95 invested in a stock and $5 in cash. Over the course of a year, the stock appreciates from $95 to $110. The NAV has increased from $100 to $115 ($110 plus $5). It is now time for distribution and the manager decides to return $5 to the investor. He could sell the stock and realize

$15 in capital gains. If he did that, there would be no return of capital. But if instead, the manager decides to hold onto the stock, he does not have any realized gains during the year so the $5 distribution is paid from his cash reserve and is considered return of capital. This is certainly not destructive since the NAV has gone up more than the $5 distribution. After the distribution, the NAV is $110.

One of the key things to know about ROC is that it has a precise definition based on tax laws. It is not necessarily the common sense definition that you would expect just based on the words. This is especially true when dealing with master limited partnerships (MLPs). Many MLPs are in the energy sector and manage oil and gas pipelines. The tax laws allow MLPs to depreciate these pipelines and this artificially reduces taxable income. So for MLPs, the cash available to distribute is usually much larger than taxable income. Because of this, CEFs that own MLPs almost always have large amounts of "good" ROC.

In summary, ROC is considered "good" or constructive if the ROC comes from pass-through events like those associated with MLPs or from unrealized capital gains. ROC is bad or destructive when an investor literally receives back their own capital as part of the distribution. Sometimes it is difficult to determine whether ROC is good or bad. My rule of thumb is that if the NAV has increased, the ROC is good. However, the reverse is not necessarily true. There could be many reasons for the NAV to decrease that have nothing to do with ROC but if the NAV is decreasing, you should delve more closely into the source of the distribution.

Total Return

The total return over a given period is the share price return plus the distribution rate. The share price return is the percentage the share price increase or decrease over the period (based on comparing the share price at the end of the period to the share price at the beginning of the period).

For example, assume you buy a CEF for $10 that has a distribution of $1 per year. After holding a year, assume that the price has increased to $11. You have gained $1 in share price and also received a $1 in distribution for a total return of $2 or 20%.

Now suppose you bought another CEF for $10 that had a distribution of $2 per year. At the end of a year, assume the CEF is now selling for $8. You have received $2 distribution but the price has declined by $2. You have no return! Even though you received a 20% distribution, your total return was zero! You should always consider the total return from an investment, not just the size of the distribution.

Managed Distributions

Some CEFs have what is called a "managed distribution" policy. This means that you receive the same monthly or quarterly distributions over the course of a year. This helps to "smooth" the distributions and enables investors to plan on how much income they will receive. This sounds like a good idea but you need to understand some of the nuances of managed distributions.

Section 19(b) of the Investment Company Act of 1940 states that it is unlawful to distribute capital gains more once per year. As we have seen, capital gains play a major role in the amount of distributions. So a number of fund companies have asked the SEC for an exemption to this 19(b) rule and most were granted. The fund company then estimates how much capital gains it will generate by the end of the year. Based on this estimate, the capital gains are spread over the monthly or quarterly distributions. This allows the funds to distribute the same amount for each distribution without having to wait until end of the year.

But forecasts can be wrong. If the manager underestimates the amount of capital gains, he will have additional funds at the end of the year and can distribute the extra funds as a "special distribution" or simply banks the excess in case the fund hits a bump down the road. If the manager overestimates the amount of capital gains, then at the end of the year, he has a shortfall which has to be made up by return of capital.

So with the managed distributions, there is a possibility of ROC from time to time as the forecasts don't quite match the actual results. As long as this is sporadic, then no worries. However, if the manger consistently overestimates the gains in order to keep the distribution high, then this would be destructive ROC and would be a reason to reassess the fund.

Why would a manager want to have a high distribution, even if it was mostly funded by destructive return of capital? Unfortunately, it is a fact of life that share prices are highly correlated with the size of the distribution. High distributions typically lead to high share prices. And many investors make their decisions based on the distribution rather than the total return. Sometimes these funds with extremely high distribution rates sell at tremendous premiums.

Take for example, Cornerstone Total Return (CRF). At the time of this writing, it has a distribution rate of over 16% and has sold for a premium as high as 44%. For the last few months, just about all this distribution has been return of capital and the NAV has been dropping. You have to decide if CRF is right for you but I would not touch it.

Important CEF Dates

There are several important dates you need to be aware of when investing in CEFs.

Record date: This is the date the fund company uses to determine who will receive a distribution. You must own the shares of the CEF on the record date to be eligible for the distribution. Since it takes 3 business days for a trade to settle, you must have purchased the CEF at least 3 days prior to the record date to be eligible for the distribution.

Ex-distribution date: On this date, the fund company will assign the distribution to the person of record. Also, on the record date the NAV will be reduced by the amount of the distribution (assuming that the assets under management do not appreciate on that day). This usually causes the share price to drop by the same amount.

Payable date: This is the date the distribution actually shows up in your brokerage account.

A Niche Market

Closed end funds are a unique investment vehicle that has characteristics between stocks and mutual funds. The closed end fund market is relatively small, with most CEFs selling only a few hundred thousand (or less) shares per day—much too small for institutions and hedge funds to trade. So about 90% of CEF's volume is from retail investors. Since CEFs are relatively complex, a talented investor can obtain an edge and make a good return without significantly increasing risks.

Summary

CEFs give you professional management, access to relatively illiquid assets, and can provide a good source of income. From time to time, you can actually purchase assets at a discount. However, the knowable investor must also take into account the volatility from leverage, the potential return of capital, and the fact that many CEFs trade at small volumes and may sometimes be difficult to buy and sell. Overall CEFs make a valuable addition to well diversified portfolios and is one of the key vehicles that will enable you to construct a "sleep soundly" portfolio.

Dr. John Dowdee

Chapter 5
Understanding Futures

You will likely never open a futures account or trade futures directly as part of your portfolio. However, many ETFs and ETNs give you access to markets that were once the province of future traders. These specialized ETFs and ETNs are often based on the futures market and can provide valuable diversification for your portfolio. Therefore, it is important to understand futures even though you will not explicitly buy or sell them.

The futures market has the reputation of being exotic and difficult to understand, but you should not be intimidated. Futures are just another way the market brings buyers and sellers together.

What is a Future?

A "future" is a promise to deliver goods on an agreed upon date in the future. The first formal futures market was established in 1697 in Osaka, Japan in the Dojima area. This was called the Dojima Rice Exchange and was established to stabilize the price of rice. Up until then, a farmer had to bring his rice crop to the city and hope to find a buyer. Because many farmers arrived at the same time, it was a chaotic process and the rice storage bins were quickly filled to overflowing. The price paid for rice was very volatile since the farmers and buyers did not have a central auction place to arrive at a fair price. Due to the fact that feudal lords were paid in rice rather than cash, the price of rice played a crucial role in the economy. In 1697, the shogunate issued a license to establish a rice exchange and the futures market was born. Farmers and merchants entered into a standard contract called Rice Coupons, which established the specific quantity, quality, and price of the rice and the time it would be delivered to the warehouse in the future. Thus, even before the rice was harvested, the farmers knew how much money they would receive and similarly, the merchants knew how much they would have to pay. The farmers could also keep the rice on their farm until it was time to deliver, which alleviated the storage overflow problem. This stabilized the price of rice and promoted commerce.

Chicago Board of Trade

The concept of future markets took hold in the United States about 150 years later when the Chicago Board of Trade (CBOT) was established in 1848. Similar to the early days in Japan, the American farmers were having a tough time finding buyers for their corn and wheat so 82 businessmen established a central buying location in Chicago. Initially, this was only a cash market (also called a spot market) where buyers and sellers would reach agreement on the spot. However, this location later evolved in a futures market with standard contacts. A standard contract is a set of rules that both buyer and seller agree to. For example, a standard wheat future contract would be:

- *Contract size: 5,000 bushels*
- *Deliverable grade: Specifies the type of wheat, for example, Number 2 Soft Red Winter Wheat*
- *Last Date for Delivery: Seventh business day after the last trading day of the delivery month. The delivery month was also standardized as March, May, July, September, or December.*
- *Price paid for the wheat. Specified to the quarter cent per bushel.*

Who Needs Futures?

Thus a farmer in Ohio might plant his wheat in September with the expectation of harvesting 100,000 bushels in July of the following year. When he planted the wheat, the price was $4 per bushel. The farmer decided that at $4 per bushel he will make a good profit but he is worried that the price may decrease before he can harvest his crop. Therefore, he hedges this price risk by selling 20 wheat contracts on the CBOT for July delivery (20 contracts times 5,000 bushels per contract is 100,000 bushels). The farmer is entering into a binding contract to deliver 100,000 bushels of Number 2 soft red winter wheat in July at an agreed upon price of $4 per bushel. In the parlance of the futures market, the farmer is short 20 contracts (he is short until he delivers). Now it does not matter to the farmer if the price of wheat increases or decreases, he knows that he will receive $4 per bushel and that his profit is locked in.

Note that the contract is legally binding and is enforced by the CBOT. If for some reason the farmer cannot deliver his agreed upon 100,000 bushels, he will have to buy wheat from another farmer to fulfill his obligation (this is not as difficult as it sounds since the CBOT has mechanisms for the farmer to buy another contract and thereby offset his commitment and close out the trade).

Who buys the farmer's wheat? Assume that in September, a cereal producer projects that he will need 100,000 bushels of wheat in July to keep his cereal production lines running. He knows that if he can buy wheat at the prevailing price of $4 a bushel, he can profit from his cereal sales. Unlike the farmer, he is worried that the price of wheat may increase. Therefore, he buys 20 contracts for delivery in July. In the parlance of the futures market, the manufacturer is long 20 contracts. Thus the farmer delivers his wheat in July and this is then transferred to the cereal manufacturer and both sides of the transaction are happy.

Commercials

In futures market, the farmer and manufacturer are called "Commercials" because they are buying or selling futures in order to hedge costs. Their primary motive from using future contracts is to reduce price volatility, so they have more certainty in their ability to make future profits. The Commercial players are the "big boys" of the future markets. They are the largest farmers or manufactures and they typically deal with large amounts of products. They also have the most knowledge of the fundamentals of their product, using their vast experience and inside information to make "life or death" decisions for the success of their farms or manufacturing plants.

In the ideal world, if a farmer wanted to hedge his crop, there would be a manufacturer ready and willing to take the other side of the transaction. However, life is never that simple. In addition to hedging, the buyer or seller of a future contract could also have a profit motive. For example, assume that wheat is selling for $4 per bushel but based on his knowledge of the market, the farmer believes that the price will increase to $4.50 by July. If this is the case, he may decide to hedge only 70,000 (14 contracts) bushels and "roll the dice" on the other 30,000 bushels (6 contracts). On the other hand, if the manufacturer has the same outlook as the farmer, he will want to lock in the lower price, so he will still want to hedge the entire 100,000 bushels. Now there is a mismatch between the Commercials. The manufacturer will need to find someone else to take the other side for 6 additional contracts—he needs a non-Commercial person willing to take the risk. This is the role of the large Speculator.

Large Speculators

The large Speculator is another one of the "big boys" but he is not a farmer or manufacturer. His goal is not to hedge anything but to make money by taking the other side of bets he believes will be profitable. The Speculator (for whatever reason) believes that wheat will decrease in price rather than increase. He therefore sells the manufacturer 6 contracts and guarantees the price of $4 a bushel. If in July when the contract comes due, wheat is selling at $3.50 a bushel, the Speculator will buy the wheat on the Spot market for $3.50 and then deliver it to the manufacturer for $4—making a quick $0.50 a bushel (or $2500 a contract) on the transaction. If the Speculator is wrong and wheat in July sells for $4.50 a bushel, then he loses $2500 a contract. Such is the life of a speculator.

If the Commercials are so smart, how can the Speculator make money? Remember that for the most part, Commercials are hedgers so their main objective is price stability rather than profiting from the transaction. Speculators take advantage of this Commercial mindset and in general, do very well in the futures market. Large speculators are large commodity funds called Commodity Trading Advisors (CTAs). They are large institutions that employ some of the best traders around. You may have heard of the Turtles and their trading acumen. Richard Dennis and William Eckhardt established a group of traders in the 1980s called the Turtles. This group used a trading system that turned $5000 into more than 100 million dollars!

Small Traders

To be a Commercials or large Speculators, you must trade a large number of contracts (the threshold is set by the commodity exchange) usually valued in the millions of dollars. Most of the retail future traders (like you or me) do not have the financial resources to trade in such quantities. These players are referred to as the Small Traders (or

60

non-reportable traders). Like Speculators, the small traders invest in future to make a profit but their transaction sizes are too small to be tracked by the exchange.

Commitment of Traders Report

The Commitment of Traders (COT) report is a report prepared weekly by the U.S. Commodity Future Trading Commission (CFTC). The CFTC was created in 1974 to regulate futures. Among other functions, the CFTC provides a summary of futures trading activity for each major player and each commodity. Some people use the report to gain insight into where the commodity market is heading and trading systems have been devised based on this data. We will not make use of the COT report for our portfolios but I have included a short description for completeness.

The report is partitioned by reportable and non-reportable positions. A reportable position is one that exceeds the reporting thresholds. For example, a market position must hold more than a 150 wheat contracts to be in the reportable category. Since one wheat contract represents 5,000 bushels, this mean that the reporting threshold is 750,000 bushels of wheat or several millions of dollars' worth of wheat. Obviously, reportable positions are held only the "big players" in a market. If a person holds less than the threshold number of contracts, they are lumped together in the non-reportable category. The CFTC sets the reportable threshold to represent from 70% to 90% of the total number of contracts in the particular commodity. The threshold may range from 25 contracts to more than a thousand contracts depending on the prevailing conditions at the time. The thresholds are reviewed periodically to see if changes are required in order to balance oversight of the market activity and burden of increased reporting documentation.

Debunking Myths about Futures

Among stock investors, futures have a bad rap because of the many misconceptions that are propagated by the financial media.

Dr. John Dowdee

Futures are extremely risky

One myth is that futures are much riskier than stocks. In fact, futures are no riskier than high volatility stocks but the reason this myth persists is because of leverage. If you use leverage, you enhance both profit and losses. A stock account allows you to buy stocks on margin (that is with borrowed money) but the amount of margin cannot exceed 100% (1 to 1) of your assets. If you open a futures account, you might be able to use leverage of 10 or 20 to 1, depending on the margin requirements associated with the commodity.

For example, you can enter into a gold contract for 100 ounces of gold with only an initial deposit of $8,800. But 100 ounces of gold may be worth $150,000 or more. Thus, to trade gold, you only have to put only about 6% of the value. This is 16 to 1 leverage! If gold prices increase by $50 per ounce, you will make $5,000 dollars—that's more than a 50% gain on your initial investment of $8,800. But now look at the flip side. Suppose gold prices decrease by $50 an ounce. Now you will lose over 50%. Gold prices can easily move more than $10 or $20 an ounce in a day and a $50 increase or decrease is not uncommon over several days. The volatility is breathtaking! If the price of gold decreased by $88 an ounce, the trader would be wiped out! This is why over 90% of futures traders go bust. This leverage is why many players are attracted by futures only to be disillusioned by the reality. Future trading is not for the faint of heart.

So if you are investing in ETFs or ETNs that use future contracts, be sure to understand how much leverage is being use. Most ETFs do not use leverage but some use as much as 300%. This amount of leverage is not large by future-trader standards but to average retail investor, price gyrations of these leveraged products can feel like a roller coaster ride.

Commodities may be delivered to your door

Another myth is that you might end up with 5,000 bushels of wheat delivered to your house (or 1000 barrels of crude, etc.). As with all myths, there is some truth. Some future traders actually want to take delivery of products, for example, a cereal maker may take delivery of grain or corn. It is only the commercial players who might consider taking delivery. Spectators do not. They close out their contracts before delivery. There is absolutely no possibility of physical deliveries when you confine your trading to ETFs and ETNs.

Summary

So to sum up, the Futures Market is the place where you can buy or sell future contracts. Each contract is a commitment to deliver a specified commodity at a specified price at a specific date in the future. To make trading easier, contacts have been standardized depending on which commodity is being traded. The easiest way for the retail investor to participate in the futures market is via ETFs and ETNs.

Dr. John Dowdee

Chapter 6
Understanding Call Options

Most individual investors have never considered trading stock options. Wall Street cloaks options with an air of complexity by talking about "Greeks" and volatility. A perception fostered by some financial advisors is that options are risky and are more akin to a Las Vegas casino than a viable stock portfolio strategy. This perception is true if you are using options to speculate, that is, attempting to make a fortune without risking much money. Speculators will likely lose all their funds, just as they would in Vegas by betting on a long shot. However, options do not have to be a gamble. Instead, if used properly, options can reduce portfolio risk and will be an important tool in your risk management toolbox.

Since most investors have not utilized options, this section will provide a basic tutorial. Understanding options is not difficult but options require a different mindset than stocks, so we will start from the beginning.

First off, options are a contract between two individuals: the person who sells the option (called the "writer") and the person who buys the option. Options do not represent ownership in anything—they are just a contract where people commit to buying or selling stocks sometime in the future. Your brokerage firm, in coordination with the option exchanges, will make sure that the person on each side of the contract fulfills their obligation.

We will limit our discussion in this book to call options and in particular covered call strategies. The sequel to this book will delve into options in more detail and demonstrate how options can be an integral part of risk management.

Call Options

If you buy a call option on a stock, you are buying the "right" but not the "obligation" to purchase that stock sometime in the future for an agreed upon price (called the "exercise price" or the "strike price").

AAPL Example

For example, assume that on 9 March, 2013 Apple (AAPL) is selling for $431.72. You believe that AAPL is undervalued and that by June of 2013, you think that AAPL will be worth at least $500 per share. There are two ways you could participate in this advance in AAPL:

- You could buy 100 shares of AAPL for $43,172 or
- You could buy an Apple 430 call that expires on 21 June 2013.

The call gives you the right, but not the obligation, to buy 100 shares of AAPL for $430 per share anytime between now and 21 June. This means that regardless of the price of AAPL, you can buy it for $430. If AAPL increases in price to $500 per share, you can still buy it for $430! It is easy to see that if AAPL is selling for $500 and you buy it for $430, you have made $70 per share or $7,000 for 100 shares! Not bad!

By buying a call option, you can make money if AAPL does in fact increase in value between now and June. So a call on AAPL has potential value. How much is it worth? That depends on the market but let's assume that your neighbor Ted doesn't believe that the AAPL will go anywhere but down. So he decides that he will sell you this option (he is called the writer of the option) for $28 a share (called the cost of the option) or $2800 for an option on 100 shares. He stipulates that the option will expire on 21 June. If Ted is correct and on the expiration date AAPL is selling for less than $430 a share, then the option to buy it at $430 a share is worthless. At this time, the option (that is the contract between you and Ted) expires and Ted pockets the $2800. However, if the price of AAPL is greater than $430 a share, you will exercise your option and Ted will have to deliver 100 shares of AAPL at $430 a share.

It is important to realize that if you buy the option, you do not actually need to have $43,000 in your bank account. If AAPL is selling for $500 a share, you can buy it from Ted at $430 and sell it immediately in the market for $500. In real life, you do not have to worry about these transactions. Your broker will buy the stock and immediately sell it. The broker will then credit your account with $500 minus $430 ($70 per share) times 100 shares, which is $7000. You did not need to have $43,000 in your account; all you needed was the original $2,800 to buy the option. Thus, for a small investment (in this case $2,800) you stand the chance of making a large amount ($7,000) in 3 months. This is a 250% return in 3 months! This is the allure that options have for speculators.

Payoff Diagrams

The profit and loss potential of options is often portrayed in a payoff diagram like the one shown in Figure 6-1, which portrays profit on the day of expiration for the buyer. As the figure illustrates, on the day of expiration, the price of the underlying stock relative to the exercise price is the key item. In the example discussed above, if on 21 June, AAPL is selling at $430 or below, the option expires worthless so the buyer has a loss equal to the cost of the option ($28 dollars in the example). If the price of AAPL is above $430, then the option begins to gain value. If the price is $431, the option is worth $1. If the price of AAPL is $458 on the expiration date, then the option is worth $28 ($458-$430). This was the price the buyer paid for the option, so this is the "breakeven" point. If the price of AAPL is higher than $458, then the buyer makes a profit on the transaction.

Call Option recap:

So this is the essence of a call option. The buyer of the call has the right, but not the obligation, to buy the stock for an agreed upon Strike Price (also called the Exercise Price). The option is valid until the agreed upon expiration date. The seller of the option gets the premium. If at the end of the expiration period the stock is above the strike price, the buyer will "exercise" the option and receive 100 shares of stock from the seller at the agreed upon price. If at the end of the expiration period, if the stock is below the strike price, the option will expire worthless and the seller will keep the premium.

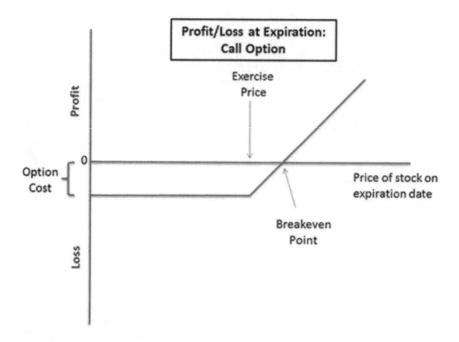

Figure 6-1: Payoff diagram for Call Options

At the risk of being redundant, I will also recap the Apple example. The buyer of the $430 AAPL calls spends $2800 to buy the option. This is his total risk—he cannot lose more than $2800. However, if AAPL does go up, he can make significantly more than $2800 (the sky is the limit as they say!). The seller on the other hand receives a guaranteed $2800. If the stock goes down, he can bank this money but if the stock goes up, he is obligated to deliver it for $430 a share (either from his account if he holds AAPL or by buying it on the open market). So if AAPL goes up substantially over the period, the seller could suffer a huge loss. For example, if APPL rocketed to $800 a share, the seller would lose $800 minus $430 ($370 per share) times 100 shares, which equals $37,000 minus the $2,800 he received for a net loss of $34,200!

Note that price of an option is always quoted in terms of one share but the contract is always in terms of 100 shares. For example, the quote for the AAPL option may say $28. But the option contract will be for 100 shares and will therefore cost you $2800.

Covered Calls

The basic idea of investing in covered calls is simple. An investor will buy a stock and write (that is sell) a call option against their stock position. Since the investor owns the stock, the position is termed "covered" and this type of transaction is allowed in most brokerage accounts. This type of strategy is also called "Buy-Write" since you buy a stock and write a call. Thus, covered calls are a way to receive additional income but in return, the writer sacrifices some of the upside potential of the stocks.

Of course, the stock could also substantially decline. The premium from the covered call will help offset losses in the stock but the entire stock-option combination could become underwater. If the investor wants to close the position, he will need to sell both the stock and the option Selling only the stock is not allowed in most accounts since this would result in the option not being covered (called a naked option), which subjects the writer to theoretically unlimited losses. Naked calls are not allowed in IRA accounts and require a high level brokerage approval in taxable accounts.

There are several ways for an investor to implement a covered call strategy. As described above, an investor may select a number of stocks and write covered calls against each of the holdings. Although simple in principle, actually implementing a profitable covered call strategy is not that easy. The investor must not only select a suitable stock but must also select the option to write (based on premium, exercise price, and time to expiration). After the covered call position is initiated, the position should be actively managed to determine when to close the position, whether or not to roll the option and to decide what type of risk management techniques to use. Don't get me wrong. Writing covered call options on individual stocks can be rewarding but it takes time and expertise. There is a much easier way. For most investors, I believe it would be advantageous to buy a professionally managed covered call fund. A detailed discussion of covered call funds will be presented in Chapter 9.

Dr. John Dowdee

Chapter 7
Evaluating Risk versus Reward

You have likely heard the old saying that you cannot achieve a significant reward without taking some risk. This sage advice is as valid in the financial markets as it is in other aspects of life. The key to successful investing is to balance these risks and rewards. In other words, you should make sure that you are adequately compensated for any risks that you taking.

Before defining risk and rewards in detail, it is important to understand that risks and rewards are personal and depends on individual situations. Some people are risk takers and can handle the financial equivalent of skydiving without worry. Other investors are more conservative and need to use both belts and suspenders to assure that their financial assets will not fall to embarrassing levels. There is not a right or wrong answer but deciding how much risk you can assume and still sleep soundly at night is an important decision you must make.

How to evaluate risk and rewards in the stock market is the subject of this chapter.

Reward (Excess Return)

Reward in the stock market is usually associated with the amount of money you make on a given investment. Stated differently, reward is the return you receive for investing a specific amount of money. For example, if you invest $100 in stock and at the end of the year, this $100 has appreciated to $110, you have received a return (or reward) of $10 or 10%. Intuitively, this is a better reward than receiving only a $5 or 5% for the year.

When investors talk of reward, they are usually referring to a special way of measuring returns called the Compound Average Growth Rate or CAGR. The idea behind CAGR is similar to the compound interest you might receive at a bank. It is a measure of the return you can receive by reinvesting dividends year over year.

As with many of the concepts in finance, CAGR is calculated by a mathematical formula that is an approximation of reality. Let's look at an example.

Suppose you start with $1000 and gain $2000 (200% gain) during the first year (way to go!). So you have $3000 at the end of the first year. You are feeling great so you let it ride. Unfortunately, the market goes south and you lose 50% during the second year. So at the end of two years, you have $1500. What is your average annual gain? It clearly is not the average arithmetic gain (200% minus 50% with the difference divided by 2 equals 75%) since making $750 each year would imply you have $2500 at the end of two years.

Using CAGR is a better way to measure your gains. The CAGR for this example can be calculated as 22.5% per year. Before looking at how this was calculated, let's see what this means. If you average 22.5% per year, after the first year you would have $1225. If this number is then multiplied by the 22.5% for the second year ($1225*1.225) the result is $1500. So this verifies that your return is 22.5% compounded annually.

Sidebar for mathematicians

To calculate CAGR you take the ratio of the ending value to the starting value, raise the ratio to the nth root where n is the number of years of compounding (in this case 2 year) and then subtract one. Let's calculate using this formula. The ratio (1500/1000) equals 1.5. Take the square root equals 1.225. Subtract 1 gives us 0.225. Converting to percentage provides a CAGR of 22.5%.

Non-Mathematicians.

If you don't like math, don't despair. There are many websites that provide an online calculator for CAGR.

For example, a calculator can be obtained at Investopedia at http://www.investopedia.com/calculator/cagr.aspx.

CAGR

CAGR is considered to be the best formula for comparing returns among different investments and will be used in this this book as the measure of the annual reward you will receive from your investment. CAGR is the number you see advertised by mutual funds touting their success. It should be noted however, that CAGR does not measure risk. In the above example, you had a CAGR of 22.5% and you might have assumed that you made 22.5% each year. As we have shown in the example, nothing could be further from the truth. You made a stupendous 200% one year but lost 50% the next year. We will discuss this volatility in a subsequent section.

Excess Return

There is one other important consideration when assessing reward. Some investments are virtually free of risk. For example, if you invest in a Certificate of Deposit (CD) from your local bank, it is insured by the Federal Deposit Insurance Corporation (FDIC) for up to $250,000. So if you invest less than $250,000, there is no risk that you will lose money; you will always receive back your investment plus interest at the end of the duration or term of the CD. However, the amount of interest you will receive is typically small (currently about 1% or less). The interest rate associated with these risk free investments is appropriately called the "risk free rate of return".

In portfolio theory, reward means the amount of return that is above the risk free rate. This is the return you achieve for taking risk. For example, if you invest in a stock and make an average return of 6% per year and the risk free return is 1%, then you have received a 5% (6% minus 1%) return for investing in a risky stock rather than sticking to an ultra-safe CD. In this book, return will be measured by the amount of money you receive over and above the risk free rate. The book will also use the words "reward" to be synonymous with "return".

So your job as a portfolio manager is to maximize the reward while you minimize the risk. Before we look at ways to achieve this objective, we have to define risk and decide how to measure it.

Risk (Volatility)

There are many ways to define risk but for this book, risk will be equated with the uncertainty about how much the value of a financial asset might change over time. An asset that experiences wild fluctuations is considered to be more "risky" than an asset that is sedate and changes slowly. This type of uncertainty is measured by a metric called "volatility".

Volatility is a measure of how much the daily return of a stock will fluctuate over a period of time, usually taken to be a year. A video on volatility can be found at:

http://www.investopedia.com/video/play/volatility/.

If you love math, you can find the formula for calculating volatility at

http://superchargeretirementincome.com/03/knowledge-center/portfolio-strategy/calculating-portfolio-risk-and-return/

However, you don't need to be a mathematician to utilize volatility in your stock selection. The rest of this section provides a heuristic explanation of volatility without resorting to anything more complex than high school math.

The higher the volatility the more uncertain you are about how the stock price will move from day to day or week to week. The price of a highly volatile stock can potentially spread over a large range of values during the year. The price change can be in either direction, either up or down. For example, biotech stocks usually have a relatively high volatility since their price may fluctuate wildly depending on the result of drug trials. Utilities, on the other hand, typically have a low volatility because their profits are regulated by municipalities.

The way volatility is defined means that most of the fluctuations of a stock's price will occur within plus or minus 2 volatilities of the average return. For example, let's say that you read an advertisement for Mutual Fund A that says that the mutual fund has gained an average of 10% per year over the past five years. When we look into the prospectus, we also find that the volatility over the 5 years has been 15% a year. If you buy the mutual fund, how much would you expect to gain over the next year? Most people would say 10% but this would be a short sighted conclusion. Based on the above data, the mutual fund should gain somewhere between the average return (10%) and plus or minus twice the volatility (2 time 15% = 30%). Thus, over the next year you would expect to gain anywhere between a loss of 20% and a gain of 40%. This is not nearly as comforting as expecting a gain of 10%. Thus if the volatility is high when compared to the average gain, there is a large amount of uncertainty and you cannot count on achieving anywhere near the average return quoted.

Let's look at another example. Assume that Mutual Fund B has an average return of 10% (the same as Mutual Fund A) but the volatility is only 5%. Now, according to probability theory, it is highly likely you will receive a gain for the year somewhere between 0% and 20%. Much better than Mutual Fund A if you are trying to make your retirement money last.

Some people don't like equating risk with volatility since volatility is bi-directional; it doesn't matter is the stock gains or loses. There are various other measures that could be used but most of these are very difficult to calculate based on historical data. Volatility is relatively easy to compute and it is used by most portfolio managers as their measure of risk.

To make it easy to assess volatility for any stock, I have provided a free Excel spreadsheet that can be downloaded from:

http://superchargeretirementincome.com/11/knowledge-center/calculator-for-excess-return-volatility-and-sharpe-ratio/.

Note that this spreadsheet uses a 3 year look-back period and also provides a calculation of the return. There is also a free calculator for volatility at http://www.InvestSpy.com.

Risk versus Reward

So now that we have defined risk as volatility and reward as average return (above the risk free rate), how do we use this data to make portfolio decisions? There are many ways to define a "good" risk to reward.

As an example, consider the SPDR S&P 500 (SPY) ETF, which is an excellent proxy for the entire stock market. Over any selected time period, SPY will have an average return and volatility. So one way to assess if the risk to reward of an investment is "good" is to compare the investment's average return and volatility to that of SPY. In other words, we can define a "good reward" as a rate of return higher than the S&P 500 and "low risk" as volatility less than the S&P 500.

You should keep in mind that the average return and volatility of the stock market depends on the time frame you are using. The reward to risk over the past year may be wildly different from the reward to risk over a longer period, like 3 years or 5 years. Just think about 2008 when the market tanked. The reward to risk during that period was horrible. However, one year later, during 2009, the reward to risk was excellent. Therefore, for any reward to risk discussion we need to define a time frame or "look-back" period. I like to use 3 years for general discussions but that is somewhat arbitrary and it depends on your objectives. For example, if you want to see how your portfolio might react during a bear market, you may want to include 2008 in your look-back period.

To summarize, to assess the reward and risk of an investment, you must first establish a look-back period that corresponds to your investment horizon. Then you choose a benchmark and compare the reward and risk of the investment relative to the benchmark. You will see many examples of this type of assessment later in the book.

Plotting Reward and Risk
Once you have the mean rate of return and volatility of each asset, you need to plot them on a Return versus Volatility (also called a reward versus risk) graph. An example graph is shown in Figure 7-1, which plots the reward and risks associated with several ETFs. This example is based on 3 years of data from September, 2011 to September, 2014.

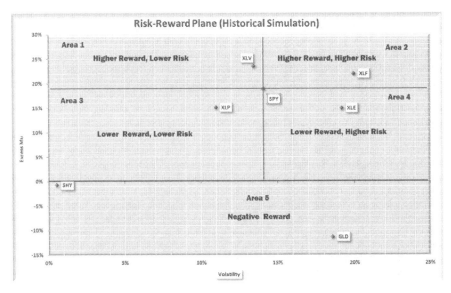

Figure 7-1. Reward versus risk plot example

In the figure, Reward is denoted as "Excess Mu". Mu is a Greek letter used to signify the average return and Excess Mu is the name use for average return above the risk free rate. In the plots that follow, Excess Mu will be synonymous with reward, which is the average return over and above the risk free rate. As we have discussed, risk is measured by the volatility.

The baseline for reward versus risk in Figure 10-1 is the SPY ETF, which is an index fund that matches the performance of the S&P 500. Other assets are measured against the reward versus risk of SPY. The reward and risk of each investment asset is plotted on the graph. The relative goodness of the asset relative to the S&P 500 depends on which area of the graph that contains the asset's risk and reward point. These areas are as follows:

Area 1: High Reward, Low Risk. Any assets that fall in Area 1 have excellent performance relative to the S&P 500. Assets in this region have generated higher return but are less risky than SPY. This is region with the best reward versus risk and assets in this region are great candidates to consider adding to your portfolio. In this example, the **Health Care Select SPDR (XLV)** falls into this area. This

Dr. John Dowdee

indicates that health care stocks (including biotech companies) have had excellent performance over the look-back period.

Area 2: High Reward, High Risk. It is more difficult to assess the relative performance of assets that fall into this region. Yes, the reward is high but so is the risk. The main question is whether or not the high return adequately compensates for the higher risk. To answer this question, will require you to evaluate another metric called the Sharpe Ratio, which will be explained later in the chapter. In this example, the **Financial Select Sector SPDR (XLF)** ETF has generated high returns but was also more risky than SPY.

Area 3: Low Reward, Low Risk. This is the mirror image of Area 2. Yes, the risk is low (which is good) but the return is also low (not so good). Does the lack of risk justify the low return? The Sharpe Ratio will also be used to refine the answer this question. The **Consumer Staples Select SPDR (XLP)** ETF falls within this region.

Area 4: Low Reward, High Risk. Assets in this area are clearly inferior to the S&P 500. The assets have lower returns than SPY but higher volatility. These assets did not lose money but they did not provide as much return as SPY and they have greater volatility. Thus, these candidates offer more risk for less reward, which is not desirable. Assets in this region are typically rejected from consideration (unless there are other over riding factors). During the 3 year period of analysis, the risk/reward associated with the **Energy Select Sector SPDR (XLE)** ETF fell into this region.

Area 5: Negative Reward. Assets that have negative rewards are not good investments regardless of the risk. We do not want to choose assets that lose money. It is true that these assets could potentially be good value plays (if they recover in the future). However, this is not the philosophy that we are using for selecting a portfolio. We want to choose candidates that have proved themselves in the past in the hopes that they will continue to outperform in the future. Of course, there are no guarantees and the adage "past performance is not an indicator of future performance" is definitely true. In this example, both the ETFs: **SPDR Gold Shares (GLD)** and **iShares 1-3 year Treasury Bond (SHY)** fell into this region.

It should be noted that SPY is not the only benchmark you can use. Suppose you wish to rank fixed income investments. In this case, it may not be appropriate to compare a bond fund with equity fund (since you expect the bond fund to have lower return and lower volatility than the overall equity stock market). In this case, it may be appropriate to use an investment grade bond fund, such as LQD, as your benchmark. Figure 7-2 shows a plot using LQD as the benchmark.

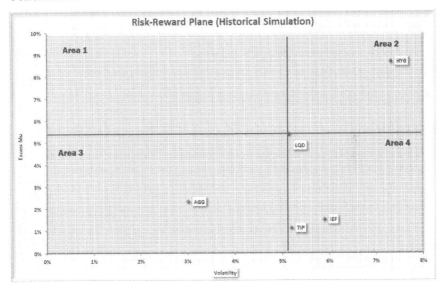

Figure 7-2 Reward versus risk for bond funds

The other ETFs on the chart are:

- **iShares Core US Aggregate Bonds (AGG)**
- **iShares iBoxx $ High Yield Corporate Bonds (HYG)**
- **iShares 7-10 Year Treasury (IEF)**
- **iShare TIPS Bond (TIP)**

This figure illustrates the power of plotting investments on the risk-reward plane. From Figure 7-2 it can easily be seen that over the period of analysis, HYG had excellent performance while the other ETFs lagged with respect to LQD.

Dr. John Dowdee

Sharpe Ratio

The Sharpe Ratio is a metric, developed by Nobel laureate William Sharpe in 1966 that measures risk-adjusted performance. It is calculated as the ratio of the average return (above the risk free rate) divided by the volatility. Thus, Sharpe Ratio measures the ratio of the Reward to Risk. This reward-to-risk ratio is a good way to compare investments to assess if higher returns are due to superior investment performance or from taking additional risk

Components of the Sharpe Ratio
The Sharpe Ratio is simple to understand and calculate.

The numerator of the Sharpe Ratio is:

Excess Mu = Annual return from investment minus risk-free return

The risk-free return is the percentage return you can obtain from a "risk-free" investment such as a bank Certificate of Deposit (CD) or a short term treasury note. Over the past few years, the risk free return has been very small. In 2014, I used 1% for the risk-free rate since this is the return I could obtain from a one year CD.

The denominator of the Sharpe Ratio is the annual volatility of the investment. Thus we have:

Sharpe Ratio = Excess Mu/Volatility

Example
Let's look at two Exchange Traded Funds:

SPDR S&P 500 (SPY). This ETF tracks the S&P 500 index and thus is a proxy for large-cap, blue-chip stocks.

iShares Russell 2000 (IWM). This ETF tracks Russell 2000 index, which is a proxy for small-cap stocks.

Figure 7-3 plots Excess Mu against volatility for SPY for the year 2013. The ETF IWM is also included on the plot to compare how small cap stocks have performed relative to the S&P 500.

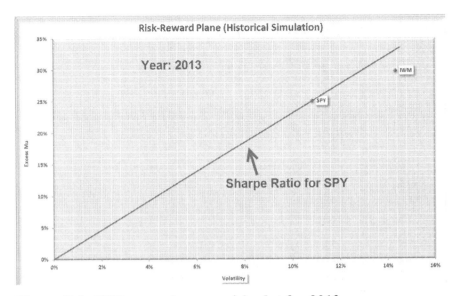

Figure 7-3: SPY reward versus risk plot for 2013

As illustrated by the chart, SPY had about a 25% Excess Mu with a volatility of 10.8%. The small cap ETF turned in a larger Excess Mu of about 30% but also had a larger volatility of 14.4%. Which is the better investment from a reward to risk perspective?

The Sharpe Ratio for SPY is 25/10.8 = 2.31. The Sharpe Ratio for IWM is 30/14.4 = 2.08. When comparing two investments, the higher the Sharpe Ratio the better. Thus, on a risk-adjusted basis, SPY has the better performance than IWM, or said another way, large-cap stocks outperformed small-cap stocks on a risk-adjusted basis.

An easy way to compare Sharpe Ratio is to draw a line between zero and the benchmark data point (in this case SPY). All points along the line have the same Sharpe Ratio. If a point is above the line, it represents a Sharpe Ratio that is better than SPY. Similarly, points below the line have a smaller Sharpe Ratio. Since the data point for IWM is below the line, it is easy to see that it has a smaller risk-adjusted return than SPY.

All metrics have both strengths and weakness, which you should understand in order to properly use the results. Here are some items to consider when using the Sharpe Ratio.

Characteristics of Sharpe Ratio

1) The Sharpe Ratio is an excellent way to separate the "wheat from the chaff" from a field of different investments.

2) The Sharpe Ratio helps investors develop strategies that match their desired return with their risk tolerance.

3) The Sharpe Ratio is conceptually simple and easy to interpret.

4) The Sharpe Ratio can be applied to assets of any type. You can compare stocks with bonds or commodities and can compare individual stocks with funds.

5) The Sharpe Ratio is available on-line at several places. One excellent source is Morningstar.com, under the "Ratings and Risk" tab for a security. You can also calculate it using the tools provided at http://www.superchargeretirementincome.com/.

6) The Sharpe Ratio provides valuable information only when compared to another investment. The absolute value of the ratio is not that important. It is the relative value that will help you choose between investments.

7) Negative Sharpe Ratios, which are plentiful during bear markets, do not provide meaningful information and should not be used. This is because the risk-free asset is providing better risk-adjusted returns than any of the negative return investments.

Using Sharpe Ratio

Figure 7-4 is the same as Figure 7-1 but now the Sharpe Ratio line is used to break Areas 2 into two Areas 2A and 2B and Area 3 into Area 3A and 3B.

Assets that fall into region 2A have Sharpe Ratios better than the SPY so should be considered for your portfolio. If an asset falls into Area 2B, the Sharpe Ratio is worse than SPY and this asset should usually be rejected (unless there are other compelling reasons to select this particular asset). Similarly, Area 3 is divided into regions 3A and 3B with area 3A representing potential candidates for inclusion and region 3B representing areas for potential rejection.

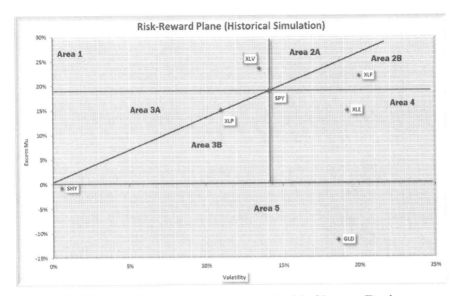

Figure 7-4 Example risk versus reward with Sharpe Ratio

In summary, all assets above the line area have Sharpe Ratios greater than the benchmark so should be considered as good candidates for inclusion in your portfolio. Assets that are below the line should most likely be rejected unless there are other compelling reasons to consider the asset.

Example: Sector ETFs

As a more comprehensive example, Figure 7-5 compares SPY with nine sector ETFs for a 3 year look-back period ending in September, 2014. The risk and reward for the following Select Sector SPRS ETFs are included on the plot:

- **SPY: S&P 500**
- **XLV: Health Care Sector**
- **XLY: Consumer Discretionary**
- **XLP: Consumer Staples**
- **XLF: Financial Sector**
- **XLE: Energy Sector**
- **XLB: Material Sector**
- **XLK: Technology Sector**
- **XLU: Utility Sector**
- **XLI: Industrial Sector**

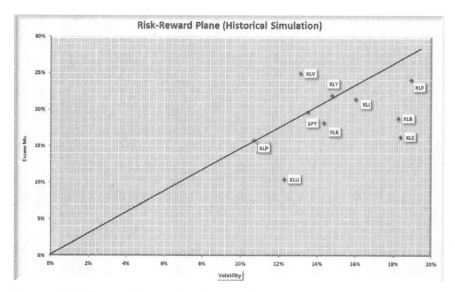

Figure 7-5 Sharpe Ratio for Sector ETFs (Sept 2011 to Sept 2014).

As you can see, by plotting the Sharpe Ratio on the Reward-Risk plane, it makes it simple to compare investment performance (in this case, over the past 3 years ending in September, 2014). From the plot, it is easy to see that the health care sector outperformed SPY, that the Consumer Discretionary and the Consumer Staples had the same risk-adjusted performance as the SPY, and all the other sectors under-performed the SPY on a risk adjusted basis.

Other Comparison Measures

This book will use Sharpe Ratio as our main tool to compare investments. However, for completeness, you should know that there are other ratios that might be used in lieu of the Sharpe Ratio. Some of the more common alternatives are:

Sortino Ratio. This is a modification of the Sharpe Ratio that differentiates "good volatility" associated with upside returns from "bad volatility" associated with downside returns. It replaces the volatility in the Sharpe Ratio with the "standard deviation of negative asset returns".

Treynor Ratio. This ratio is similar to the Sharpe Ratio but uses the beta of an investment instead of the volatility.

Calmar Ratio. This ratio is a measure of the risk-adjusted return of an investment portfolio. It is calculated as the average excess return earned by a portfolio over the last 36 months divided by maximum drawdown for the past 36 months

Summary

The Reward versus Risk plot and the Sharpe Ratio are powerful tools for assessing the relative performance of investments. If an investment is above the Sharpe Ratio line, it had a better risk-adjusted performance than the benchmark. Conversely, if an investment is below the Sharpe Ratio line, the risk-adjusted performance is poorer than the benchmark. We will make extensive use of this Risk-Reward plane and Sharpe Ratio in the later chapters.

Dr. John Dowdee

Chapter 8
Asset Allocation and Diversification

Asset allocation is a technique that attempts to balance reward versus risk by diversifying your portfolio among different sectors of the market. For many people, asset allocation means choosing among bonds, domestic stocks, and international stocks. But this just scratches the surface of possible ways to diversify. This book casts a wide net that includes non-traditional sectors such as commodities, precious metals, currencies, real estate trusts, and master limited partnerships. We will first discuss diversification and then show how your assessment of diversification can help you allocate your funds among assets.

Diversification

Basically, diversification is "not placing all your eggs in one basket". If you are diversified, then when one of your investments goes down, you hope another will go up to offset your loss.

Note that diversification does not generally boost performance—it won't prevent losses or guarantee gains. However, if you are diversified, you reduce the risk of having large losses (but in the same manner, it will also reduce the opportunity for large gains). This will smooth out the ups and downs of your portfolio, which generally is a good investment strategy (it allows you to sleep soundly without having to unduly worry about your portfolio).

Let's take an example. Let's assume that you observe that the price of gold bullion usually moves opposite to the stock market. If the market goes up, the price of gold usually goes down. If the market goes down, then gold increases in value. Thus if you add gold to your portfolio, you are becoming more diversified.

Correlation

Correlation is at the heart of diversification. Correlation tells you how consistently data, for example, stock prices, move together. If the price of Stock A always increases when the price of Stock B increases, the stock prices are said to be positively correlated. If on the other hand, the price of Stock A decreases when the price of Stock B increases, then the stock prices are said to be negatively correlated. If there is no consistent pattern between the stock prices of Stock A and Stock B, they are said to be uncorrelated.

Correlation is a number between -100% and +100% and is computed based on the historical prices of assets being compared. It tells you "on average" how often the two assets move together. If Stocks A and Stock B have a correlation of -70%, this says that 70% of the time they are moving in opposite directions. Similarly, if the correlation was +80% then, 80% of the time the stocks would be moving in the same direction.

The degree of correlation is sometimes counterintuitive. Some people buy large-cap, mid-cap, and small-cap mutual funds and believe they are diversified. This may not be the case. In many cases, these assets could be highly correlated with one another and this will kill your hopes of diversification. You cannot guess at correlation. You must calculate it.

You can obtain a free calculation of correlation between two stocks at http://www.macroaxis.com or http://www.InvestSpy.com.

So the question: "Are you diversified?" is the same as the question: "Are your assets correlated?"

Correlation FAQs

Below are a few Frequently Asked Questions (FAQs) that debunk some of the myths about correlation.

1) Is the correlation constant between two stocks? No. The correlation is constantly changing. If you use 30 days' worth of data to calculate correlation, you will get a different answer than if you used 180 days. This makes diversification more of an art than a science. In our portfolios, we typically use 3 years' worth of data so we are assessing

long term correlation. This could be substantially different from short term correlation.

2) Does correlation imply causality? Absolutely not. If A and B are positively correlated, this does not mean that the increase in A CAUSES the increase in B. Correlation is just an observation that when A increases then B seems to increases—no causality is implied. Here is an example that illustrates this lack of causality. Assume that you collect data on all the fires in Los Angeles, California. For each fire, you keep track of the damage done and the number of fire engines that responded to the fire. You find that when there are a large number of fire engines at a fire, then the amount of damage tends to be high. Thus, the number of fire engines is positively correlated with the total damage from the fire! However, it is ludicrous to think that the larger number of fire engines caused the damage to increase.

3) Does correlation measure all the relationships between two sets of data? No. Correlation is only a good measure of the linear relationship between two sets of data. If the data are related by a more exotic relationship (exponentially, squared, cubed, etc.) then correlation is not a good measure of relationship.

Asset Allocation

Asset allocation is one of the most critical decisions you can make when developing your investment strategy. Bogle, in his 1994 book, *Bogle on Mutual Funds*, indicated that asset allocation accounted for over 90% of the difference between the returns recorded by pension funds. To understand the importance of asset allocation, we need to first take an excursion into Modern Portfolio Theory.

More Gain with Lower Risk

Modern Portfolio Theory (MPT) was developed over 50 years ago by Harry Markowitz. It was first published in a 1952 article on *"Portfolio Selection"* and later in 1959 in his book *"Portfolio Selection: Efficient Diversification of Investments"*. The theory itself is very mathematical and is based on some assumptions that are only approximately true in the real world. For our purposes, we do not need to delve into the intricacies of the math but instead, we just need an overall appreciation of what Markowitz was saying. Incidentally, Markowitz won the Nobel Prize in Economics in 1990 for this work.

Modern Portfolio Theory provides a method for investors to lower the risk of their investment without lowering the return. The fundamental premise behind MPT is that investors should not choose assets for a portfolio based entirely on their anticipated returns. Instead, it is important to consider how each investment changes in price relative to the other assets. In other words, it is important to take correlation into account.

Let's look at a simple example. Suppose you buy stocks in two oil companies and these stocks move together in unison. Assume that if Stock A increases by 5% then stock B will also increase by 5% and that the same is true for decreases. These stocks are said to be perfectly correlated and have a correlation coefficient of one (which is the same as 100%). It is easy to see that you do not get any diversification by owning both of these stocks. You might as well buy twice as much of stock A and forget about Stock B.

Now suppose you buy a jewelry store stock and a gold mining stock. For the sake of illustration, assume that if the price of the gold mining stock increases, then the jewelry store stock always decreases. These stocks are said to be perfectly negatively correlated. Also assume for this example that the jewelry stock has appreciated at an average rate return of 10% a year. Of course, it does not return exactly 10% each year, some years it returns more and other years less. As discussed in the previous chapter, the measure of uncertainty is called the volatility. Assume the jewelry stock has a volatility of 10%. Assume also that the gold mining stock has a slightly higher return, averaging 13% but is much riskier, with a volatility of 30%.

An Amazing Observation
Which of these stocks would you buy? If we use the Sharpe Ratio defined in the previous chapter, the jewelry stock has a Sharpe Ratio of 10/10= 1. The gold mining stock has a Sharpe Ratio of 13/30 =0.43. So on a risk-adjusted basis, the jewelry stock is a much better performer and should be the stock selected unless there is a compelling reason (other than Sharpe Ratio) to purchase the gold mining stock. In this case, the compelling reason is that the gold miner is perfectly negatively correlated with the jewelry stock. If we

combine these two stocks into a portfolio, with some percentage of total funds allocated to the jewelry stock and the rest of the funds allocated to the gold miner, then the surprising results are shown in Figure 8-1.

Type of Stock	Return	Volatility			
Jewelry Store Stock	10%	10%			
Gold Mine Stock	13%	30%			
Type of Stock	Portfolio #1 (% of funds allocated)	Portfolio #2 (% of funds allocated)	Portfolio #3 (% of funds allocated)	Portfolio #4 (% of funds allocated)	Portfolio #5 (% of funds allocated)
Jewelry Store Stock	100%	75%	50%	25%	0%
Gold Mine Stock	0%	25%	50%	75%	100%
Return for Portfolio	10%	10.70%	11.50%	12.30%	13%
Volatility of Portfolio	10%	0%	10%	20%	30%

Figure 8-1 Return and volatility of portfolios

The table above indicates what would happen if you bought both these stocks in the percentages shown. The calculations used to generate this table are relatively complex and are outside the scope of this book. However, you don't need to understand the math to understand the underlying principle.

Look closely at the table and you will see something an amazing result. If you combine 75% of the jewelry store stock together with 25% of the gold mining stock (Portfolio #2), you will receive on average 10.7% return (see row Return for Portfolio) but with absolutely no risk! Let me repeat, the volatility is zero. The reason you do not have any risk is that the two stocks are perfectly negatively correlated, something that would be very hard to find in real life. This hard to believe fact was discovered by Markowitz and it won him the Nobel Prize.

If you are like me, you are now wondering: how do I construct a portfolio that will have great returns with no risk? As you might expect, it is not possible in the real world. This example was concocted just to illustrate the point. Unfortunately, you cannot find investments that are perfectly negatively correlated and both have positive returns. You can buy inverse ETFs but if one has a positive return then the other will have negative returns. However, the figure illustrates one of the key tenets of Modern Portfolio Theory:

Key tenet: You can reduce the overall risk of a portfolio by including a mix of investments that are not highly correlated with each other. The less the correlation among the investments the more diversification you achieve. The more diversification the lower the composite risk.

Real World Implementation

It is difficult to accept that adding a risky asset to your portfolio can actually reduce your overall risk but that is the quest of sophisticated portfolio managers. In the real world, you cannot find a portfolio that will allow you to achieve gains at no risk. But by choosing assets based on their correlation, you will develop a diversified portfolio that will allow you to lower risks and still maintain a good return.

Assessing the diversification of a portfolio and the effects on risk is more of an art than a science (unless you want to tackle portfolio math). However, if you choose assets that are not highly correlated with one another, you can rest assured that you will be obtaining diversification benefits. By taking the time to check correlations, you will reduce risks.

That being said, you would think all investors would embrace MPT and look for uncorrelated assets. Sadly this is not the case, due in large part to the lack of uncorrelated assets recommended by your brokerage firm. Stocks of all stripes, even international stocks, have become more and more correlated as globalization has taken hold. Brokerage firms have been reluctant to promote non-traditional asset classes. This was once due to difficulty of finding uncorrelated assets. However, the advent of ETFs and ETNs has changed all of that. In Part II of this book, you will see how to utilize these ETFs and ETNs to supercharge your portfolio. You will need to be proactive and search out opportunities. Take your cue from institutional investors and hedge funds that have long practiced the tenets of MPT.

Part II
Exploring Non-traditional Assets to Spice Up Your Portfolio

Chapter 9: Covered Call Funds

Chapter 10: Real Estate Investment Trusts (REIT) Funds

Chapter 11: Master Limited Partnership (MLP) Funds

Chapter 12: Commodity and Agricultural Funds

Chapter 13: Precious Metal Funds

Chapter 14: Currency Funds

Important Notice

To fit the requirements of this book, the figures had to be reduced in size and printed in black and white. To view the charts in full size and in color, please go to www.SuperchargeRetirementIncome.com and click on Book Charts or follow the link below

http://superchargeretirementincome.com/02/knowledge-center/supercharge-retirement-income-charts-for-book/

Dr. John Dowdee

Chapter 9
Enhancing Income by Using Covered Call Funds

In chapter 6, we discussed Call options. This chapter shows how funds may enhance their income by selling call options on stocks the fund already owns. This is called a covered call strategy and has worked well in past.

The mechanics of using covered call was covered in Chapter 6 so will not be repeated here. Suffice it to say that covered calls are a way to receive additional income but for receiving this income, the writer sacrifices some of the upside potential of the stocks. In a strong bull market, you would expect the covered call strategy to under-perform the SP 500 because many of the best performing stocks will be "called away". But during a correction, the premium provides a buffer to limit losses so, theoretically, writing covered calls should decrease volatility. This is not always true since volatility is dependent on the specific strategy implemented by the writer. This strategy can also be generalized to selling options on an "index" (like the S&P 500) rather than an individual stock.

Writing covered call options on individual stocks can be rewarding but it is not for the "buy and forget" investor. I believe that for most investors it would be advantageous to buy a professionally managed covered call fund. There are two types of funds that offer covered call portfolios: Closed End Funds (CEFs) and Exchange Traded Funds (ETFs).

Covered Call CEFs

Covered calls have been available to individual investors for a long time but were not embraced by funds until relatively recently. In 2002, the Chicago Board of Options Exchange (CBOE) launched the BuyWrite Index (BXM) based on selling near-term, near-the-money options on the S&P 500 index. Back testing this index showed that it often outperformed the S&P 500 with less risk (as measured by the volatility). This result generated interest in the investment community and in 2004 the first covered call CEF was offered by the Blackrock fund managers (the Enhanced Capital and Income Fund). More offerings followed swiftly and today there are over 30 covered call CEFs. To be classified as a covered call fund, call options must be written on more than 50% of the fund's assets.

By selling calls to augment income plus using leverage, the covered call CEFs often provide large distributions. However, to put these high yields in proper perspective, you have to make sure that these are "true yields" and not just return of your capital (ROC). Determining if ROC is "bad" or "good" is not as easy as you might think for covered call CEFs because ROC is based on definitions in the corporate tax code and is not necessarily synonymous with return of principal. However, if over the course of a year, the Net Asset Value (NAV) increases, then the fund earned more (either by income or capital gains) than it distributed and the distribution should not be considered destructive. Therefore, looking at total return rather than distributions is a much better way of appraising covered call CEFs.

There are currently 30 covered call funds listed on http://www.CEFConnect.com. To reduce my sample size, I used the following selection criteria.

- I wanted to analyze covered call CEFs over a 3 year period so the CEF must have a history back to at least October, 2011.
- The CEFs had to be liquid, with an average trading volume of at least 50,000 shares per day.
- The Market Capitalization had to be at least $300 million.

Based on these criteria, I reduced the number of CEFs to the following 12 CEFs. The data below was valid as of October, 2014 but may change significantly due to market conditions. Before investing in any CEF, you should review the most recent data at the CEFConnect website referenced above or check http://www.morningstar.com.

Analysis of closed end funds is also covered at http://www.superchargeretirementincome.com and at

http://www.seekingalpha.com.

Blackrock Global Opportunity (BOE). This CEF typically sells for a discount of about 10% to 11%. This fund has 135 holdings, spread over all caps, with about 50% domiciled in the United States. The other major geographic areas for investment are the United Kingdom and Japan. The fund does not utilize leverage and has an expense ratio of 1.1%. The distribution usually ranges from 8% to 9%, with a large portion coming from non-destructive ROC.

BlackRock Enhanced Capital and Income (CII). This is the oldest covered call CEF with an inception date of 2004. It typically sells at a discount of 8% to 10%. This fund is relatively concentrated, with only about 60 holdings, with most invested in U.S. companies. The managers have a flexible mandate and can invest in all size companies but most are medium to large caps. The fund does not use leverage and has an expense ratio of 0.9%. The distribution is about 8.7%, with a significant portion coming from non-destructive ROC.

Eaton Vance Enhanced Equity Income (EOI). This fund typically sells at a discount of 8% to 11%. The fund holds about 70 securities all from the United States. The fund does not use leverage and has an expense ratio of 1.1%. The distribution is usually about 8% consisting of income plus some non-destructive ROC.

Eaton Vance Enhanced Equity Income II (EOS). This sister fund to EOI typically sells at a discount of 7% to 10%. The fund has about 75 holdings, all from the United States and has a focus on technology stocks. The fund does not use leverage and has an expense ratio of 1.1%. The distribution is usually about 7% to 8%, consisting primarily of long term gains and non-destructive ROC.

Eaton Vance Risk-Managed Diversified Equity Income (ETJ). This CEF typically sells for a discount of between 8% and 11%. The fund contains about 75 large cap stocks focused on technology, financials, healthcare, consumer discretionary, and energy. Most of the holdings are U.S. based companies. This fund has a unique option strategy—selling calls and using part of the income to buy puts. The puts insulate the fund during down markets (it only lost 6% in 2008) but holds back performance in bull markets. The fund does not use leverage and has an expense ratio of 1.1%. The fund has used destructive ROC in the past but currently the 10% distribution is paid largely from non-destructive ROC.

Dr. John Dowdee

Eaton Vance Tax--Managed Buy-Write Opportunities (ETV).
This CEF typically sells at a discount of 6% to 7%. This is a large
fund with over 200 holdings, all from the United States. About 60%
of the holdings are from S&P 500 stocks and the other 40% are from
NASDAQ stocks. The managers have the discretion to overweight
some areas if they feel it will enhance returns. The name "tax-
managed" means that the fund managers try to minimize the tax
burden by periodically selling stocks that have incurred losses and
replacing them with similar holdings. This strategy has the effect of
reducing or delaying taxable gains. The fund does not use leverage
and has an expense ratio of 1.1%. The distribution is usually about
9%.

**Eaton Vance Tax-Managed Global Buy-Write Opportunities
(ETW).** This CEF typically sells at a discount of 8% to 10%. This is
a large fund with over 450 holdings, with about 55% from U.S. firms.
After the United States, the largest holdings are from the United
Kingdom and Japan. The fund does not use leverage and the expense
ratio is 1.1%. The distribution is usually 9% to 10%, paid primarily
from non-destructive ROC.

Eaton Vance Tax-Managed Dividend Equity Income (ETY). This
CEF typically sells for a discount of between 8% and 10%. The fund
has about 75 holdings with 90% from the North American region. The
rest of the holdings are primarily domiciled in Europe. The fund
typically writes options on the S&P 500 index rather than individual
stocks. The fund does not use leverage and has an expense ratio of
1.1%. The distribution is usually about 9%, consisting primarily of
income and non-destructive ROC.

Eaton Vance Tax-Managed Global Fund (EXG). This CEF
typically sells at a discount of 5% to 6%. The fund has over 200
holdings with calls written against domestic and international indexes
instead of individual stocks. The fund does not use leverage and has
an expense ratio of 1.1%. The distribution is usually about 7% to 8%,
consisting primarily of non-destructive ROC.

ING Global Equity Dividend and Premium Opportunities (IGD).
This CEF typically sells at a discount between 4% and 7%. The fund
has about 100 global holdings with 50% from the United States and
Canada, 40% from Europe, and 10% from Asia. The fund managers

98

have a flexible mandate that allows them to invest in individual stock options or index options. The fund does not use leverage and has an expense ratio of 1.2%. The distribution is usually about 10%, paid primarily from income, capital gains, and non-destructive ROC.

Nuveen Equity Premium Opportunities (JSN). This CEF typically sells at a discount of 6% to 8%. The fund has over 200 holdings, all from the United States. The fund usually selects about 75% of its holdings from the S&P 500 and the rest from the NASDAQ. This fund does not use leverage and has an expense ratio of 1%. The distribution is about 8%, paid primarily from income and non-destructive ROC.

NFJ Dividend Interest and Premium (NFJ). This CEF typically sells at a discount of 4% to 6%. The fund has about 150 holdings, with most from North America. The fund has a unique strategy that invests 75% in equities and 25% in convertible bonds. The largest sector allocations are energy, financials, healthcare, and basic materials. The fund does not use leverage and has an expense ratio of 1%. The distribution is usually about 10%, paid primarily from income and non-destructive ROC.

Covered Call Exchange Traded Funds

The only liquid covered call ETF that has a long history is summarized below.

PowerShares S&P 500 BuyWrite (PBP). This ETF tracks the CBOE S&P 500 BuyWrite Index, which measures the return received by buying the 500 stocks in the S&P 500 and selling a succession of one-month, near-the-money S&P 500 index call options. The fund has an expense ratio of .75% and yields 5.1%. This ETF was launched in December of 2007 so its data does not quite span the entire bear-bull cycle.

Reference ETF

The S&P 500 will be used for reference so we can compare the performance of the covered calls with the general stock market. The ETF used for comparison is:

SPDR S&P 500 (SPY). This ETF tracks the S&P 500 equity index and has a yield of 1.8% and an expense ratio of 0.09%.

Analysis of Candidates

Now that you have a listed of potential covered call funds for your portfolio, you need to check the correlation to see if they will provide a reasonable degree of diversification. As discussed in Chapter 8, selecting assets based on correlations is more art than a science. Generally, I do not like to select two assets if the correlation is above 80% since I would not receive adequate diversification. Any correlations lower than 80% are fine but the lower the better.

Correlation of Covered Call Funds

The correlations for the covered calls over a 3 year period (from October, 2011 to October, 2014) are shown in Figure 9-1. If the look-back period changes, then the correlations will also change but we will standardize on 3 years unless there is a compelling reason to look at other time frames.

Correlation Matrix

	BOE	CII	EOI	EOS	ETJ	ETV	ETW	ETY	EXG	IGD	JSN	NFJ	PBP	SPY
BOE	1.000													
CII	0.761	1.000												
EOI	0.806	0.827	1.000											
EOS	0.767	0.781	0.903	1.000										
ETJ	0.725	0.735	0.798	0.768	1.000									
ETV	0.763	0.797	0.845	0.807	0.765	1.000								
ETW	0.790	0.792	0.862	0.825	0.768	0.827	1.000							
ETY	0.809	0.791	0.874	0.836	0.787	0.815	0.872	1.000						
EXG	0.799	0.777	0.851	0.813	0.757	0.800	0.867	0.906	1.000					
IGD	0.743	0.687	0.758	0.732	0.666	0.741	0.774	0.757	0.762	1.000				
JSN	0.699	0.758	0.763	0.744	0.698	0.774	0.747	0.743	0.704	0.682	1.000			
NFJ	0.660	0.693	0.704	0.672	0.621	0.667	0.711	0.710	0.688	0.672	0.664	1.000		
PBP	0.687	0.714	0.758	0.722	0.667	0.700	0.737	0.721	0.720	0.629	0.625	0.617	1.000	
SPY	0.781	0.800	0.865	0.810	0.752	0.790	0.824	0.832	0.819	0.691	0.705	0.655	0.857	1.000

Figure 9-1. Correlation matrix for 3 year period ending October, 2014

The figure illustrates what is called a correlation matrix. The symbols for the covered call CEFs are listed in the first column on the left side of the figure along with SPY for reference. The symbols are also listed along the first row at the top. The number in the intersection of the row and column is the correlation between the two assets. For example, if you follow EOS to the right for two columns you will see that the intersection with CHI is 0.781. This indicates that, over the 3 year period, EOS and CHI were 78.1% correlated. Note that all assets are 100% correlated with itself so the diagonal of the matrix are all ones. The last row of the matrix allows us to assess the correlations of the CEFs with SPY.

There are several observations from the correlation matrix.

- Most of the covered call CEFs are relatively highly correlated (greater than 80%) with SPY. Thus if you have an equity portfolio that mimics the S&P 500, then you may not want to purchase the covered call CEFs that are highly correlated (EOI, EOS, ETW, ETY, EXG, or PBP)
- The CEFs that have the lowest correlation with SPY are BOE, CHI, ETJ, ETV, IGD, and NFJ. Thus, if you have a general equity portfolio, these CEFs may be your best choice.
- If your portfolio is more exoteric and does not reflect the S&P 500, then you are free to select any of the covered call funds. Generally, it is OK to purchase more than one of the CEFs if they are not highly correlated with each other. However, it pays to check the pair-wise correlation before you make a final decision. For example, you would not want to purchase both EOS and EOI since these two CEFs are over 90% correlated.

Reward versus Risk of Covered Call Funds

The next step in our analysis is to plot the reward versus risk for each of these CEFs. This plot is shown in Figure 9-2 where the excess return (called Excess Mu on the chart) is plotted against volatility. This plot uses the same 3 year look-back period as the correlation matrix. The "line" shows the Sharpe Ratio associated with SPY. If an asset is above the line, it has a better risk-adjusted return than the S&P 500. Similarly, if as asset is below the line, the associated risk-adjusted return is poorer than SPY.

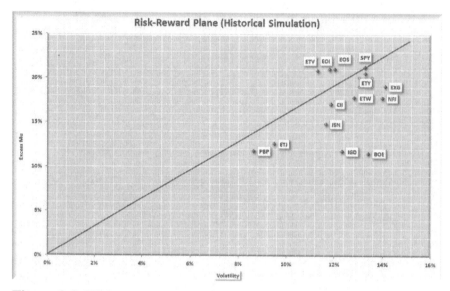

Figure 9-2. Risk versus reward over 3 years ending October, 2014

Some interesting observations are evident from the figure.

- Over the 3 year analysis period, the majority of covered call CEFs had absolute returns less than SPY. This is not surprising since the S&P 500 had been in a rip roaring bull market over the look-back period.
- Most of the CEFs had a lower volatility than SPY. This is what you would expect with covered calls. However, a few have volatilities that exceeded SPY. This is likely due to the nature of closed end funds, since the fluctuations associated with discounts tend to increase volatility.
- The lowest risk covered call asset is the PBP. This is not surprising since ETFs are passive and follow an index. CEFs are actively managed where the managers try to beat the passive indexes but this typically increases volatility.

- In terms of risk-adjusted performance, ETV, EOI, and EOS all beat SPY. Based on this performance, ETV would be a good candidate to add to a general market portfolio since ETV is not highly correlated with SPY. However, I would only purchase one of the CEFs since the three funds are highly correlated with one another.
- Another potential purchase might be NFJ. This CEF has the least correlation with SPY and is also relatively uncorrelated with the other CEFs. NFJ does not have the best risk-adjusted performance but the performance has been relatively good.

Summary

The analysis of Covered Call funds has illustrated how correlations and risk/reward plots can be used to narrow down a list of candidates. This allowed us to select several candidates that would increase the diversification of a general equity portfolio. Over the 3 years associated with the look-back period, ETV and NFJ appeared to be good candidates. You may be reading this book during a much different time frame, so you should perform your own evaluation and due diligence using the techniques discussed in this book.

As always, past performance may not be a good predictor of future returns and volatility but I believe that risk-tolerant retirees should consider covered call funds for their income portfolio. The covered call funds have outstanding distributions and offer good (but not great diversification). You would not expect this asset class to excel in a bull market but some of the funds have held their own with respect to the S&P 500.

Dr. John Dowdee

Chapter 10
Real Estate Investment Funds (REITs)

Historically, Real Estate Investment Trusts (REITs) have been a favorite asset class for income oriented investors. REITs were hit hard in the 2008 bear market but have rebounded strongly along with other equities since the 2009 low. The fundamentals associated with the REIT sector are strong but if interest rates rise, there could be significant headwinds. To understand the factors that affect REIT prices, the next section will provide a tutorial on this asset class.

REIT Tutorial

In 1960, Congress created a new type of security call a REIT that allowed real estate investments to be traded as a stock. The objective of this landmark legislation was to provide a way for small investors to participate in the income from large scale real estate projects. A REIT is a company that specializes in real estate, either through properties or mortgages. There are two major types of REITs

- Equity REITs purchase and operate real estate properties. Income usually comes through the collection of rents. About 90% of REITs are equity REITs.
- Mortgage REITs invest in mortgages or mortgage backed securities. Income is generated primarily from the interest that is earned on mortgage loans.

The risks and rewards associated with mortgage REITs are very different from those associated with equity REITs. This chapter will only consider equity REITs since mortgage REITs are notoriously risky.

One of the reasons REITs are so popular is that they receive special tax treatment and as a result, are required to distribute at least 90% of their taxable income each year. This usually translates into relatively large yields. But because REITs must pay out 90% of their income, they rely on debt for growth. This means that REITs are sensitive to interest rates. If the interest rates rise, the cost of debt increases and the REIT has less money for business investment. However, on the plus side, rising rates usually implies increased economic activity and as the economy expands, there is a higher demand for real estate, which bodes well for REITs.

Rather than investing in individual REITs, I prefer REIT funds. This next sections reviews both CEFs and ETFs that invest in REITs and analyzes the risk versus rewards associated with these funds.

REIT Closed End Funds

As an income investor, I am a fan of Closed End Funds (CEFs) due to their large distributions. There are currently 11 CEF funds focused on REITs. To narrow the analysis space, I used the following selection criteria:

- A history that goes back at least 3 years
- A market cap of at least $200M
- An average daily trading volume of at least 50,000 shares
- The following 6 CEFs met all of my selection criteria.

Nuveen Real Estate Income (JRS). This CEF typically sells at about a 4% premium but from time to time it will sell at a discount. The fund has about 85 holdings spread over all types of REITs (residential, commercial, retail). It utilizes 30% leverage and has an expense ratio of 1.8%, including interest payments. This distribution is usually 8% to 9%, some of which may be return of capital (ROC).

Neuberger Berman Real Estate Securities Income (NRO). This CEF typically sells for a large discount between 12% and 15%. The fund consists of 65 holdings with 75% in diversified REITs and 30% in the preferred shares. The fund uses leverage of 25% and has an expense ratio of 2.1%, including interest payments. The distribution is 5% but comes directly from income with no ROC.

Cohen Steers Quality Income Realty (RQI). This CEF typically sells at a discount between 7% and 10%. The fund has about 130 holdings consisting of REITs (82%) and preferred stock (16%). The fund utilizes 25% leverage and has an expense ratio of 2%, including interest payments. The distribution is usually between 7% and 8%, consisting primarily of income and long term gains with very little ROC.

Cohen Steers Total Return Realty (RFI). This CEF typically sells at a discount of between 1% and 5%. The fund has about 160 holdings with 88% in REITs and about 10% in preferred shares. The fund does not use leverage and has an expense ratio of 0.9%. The distribution is usually about 8% with no ROC.

Cohen and Steers REIT and Preferred (RNP). This CEF typically sells for discount between 8% and 12%. The portfolio consists of about 200 holding with 52% in REITs and 47% in preferred shares. The fund uses 26% leverage and has an expense ratio of 1.8%, including interest payments. The distribution is usually about 7.6%, consisting primarily of income with some ROC.

CBRE Clarion Global Real Estate I (IGR). This CEF typically sells for a discount of between 9% and 12%. The portfolio consists of about 60 securities with 95% in REITs and the rest in preferred shares. About 50% of the holdings are from the United States with the rest spread over Asia, Europe, Australia, and Canada. This fund utilizes only a small amount of leverage (5%) and has a relatively small expense ratio of 1%. The distribution is usually about 6.5%, consisting of income and ROC.

Alpine Global Premier Property (AWP). This CEF typically sells for a discount between 10% and 11%. The portfolio consists of about 110 holdings with almost all (95%) in REITs. Only 32% of the holdings are domiciled in the United States. The next largest geographical weightings are Japan at 15%. The fund uses only a small amount (9%) of leverage and has an expense ratio of 1.3%, including interest payments. The distribution is usually about 8% to 9%, consisting primarily of income and ROC.

REIT Exchange Traded Funds

There are currently about 6 REIT ETFs that are liquid (volume over 50,000 shares per day on average). The Vanguard REIT (VNQ) is by far the largest and most liquid. The other 5 ETFs listed below were not included in the analysis because they are 99% correlated with VNQ. This often happens when ETFs track the same or similar indexes.

- **iShares Dow Jones US Real Estate (IYR)**
- **iShares Cohen& Steers Realty Majors (ICF)**
- **SPDR Dow Jones REIT (RWR)**
- **Schwab U.S. REIT (SCHH)**
- **First Trust S&P REIT Index (FRI)**

The Vanguard ETF is summarized below.

Vanguard REIT Index (VNQ). This ETF tracks the MSCI US REIT Index, which is a pure equity REIT index. The index is diversified across real estate sectors with retail being the largest constituent at 27% followed by Office (15%), residential (15%), and health care (15%) REITs. The fund charges a minuscule 0.10%, which is substantially less than most of its competitors. The fund typically yields about 3.5 %.

Reference ETFs

The S&P 500 will be used for reference so we can compare the performance of REITs with the general stock market. The ETF used for comparison is:

SPDR S&P 500 (SPY). This ETF tracks the S&P 500 equity index and has a yield of 1.8% and an expense ratio of 0.09%.

Analysis of Candidates

Now that you have a list of potential REIT funds, you need to check the correlation to see if they will provide a reasonable degree of diversification. As discussed in Chapter 8, selecting assets based on correlations is more art than science but generally, I like to select assets that have correlation lower than 80%.

REIT Correlation

The correlations for the REIT funds over a 3 year period (from October, 2011 to October, 2014) are shown in Figure 10-1. Depending on your investment horizon, you could choose a longer or shorter look-back period but this book will standardize on 3 years.

Correlation Matrix									
	AWP	IGR	JRS	NRO	RFI	RNP	RQI	VNQ	SPY
AWP	1.000	0.68	0.52	0.65	0.49	0.63	0.63	0.53	0.67
IGR	0.681	1.000	0.56	0.66	0.52	0.68	0.72	0.68	0.60
JRS	0.517	0.557	1.000	0.56	0.42	0.55	0.61	0.60	0.50
NRO	0.653	0.664	0.564	1.000	0.57	0.69	0.74	0.79	0.66
RFI	0.494	0.517	0.425	0.567	1.000	0.54	0.59	0.55	0.46
RNP	0.628	0.682	0.553	0.693	0.537	1.000	0.74	0.68	0.57
RQI	0.628	0.718	0.614	0.740	0.591	0.738	1.000	0.73	0.62
VNQ	0.629	0.679	0.595	0.786	0.550	0.679	0.734	1.000	0.78
SPY	0.667	0.600	0.498	0.665	0.460	0.566	0.620	0.780	1.000

Figure 10-1 Correlation over 3 years

There are several conclusions that are evident from the correlation matrix.

- REIT CEFs offer excellent diversification to a general market portfolio with correlations less than 70%.
- The Vanguard ETF (VNQ) is the most highly correlated at 78% but this is still below our threshold of 80%.
- The REIT funds are not very correlated with each other so it would be fine to add more than one fund to your portfolio.
- JRS exhibits some of the lowest correlations, usually below 60%.

Reward versus Risk REIT Funds

The next step in our analysis is to plot the reward versus risk of each of these funds. This plot is shown in Figure 10-2 where the excess return (called Excess Mu) on the chart is plotted against volatility. This plot uses the same 3 year look-back period as the correlation matrix. The look-back period is from October, 2011 to October, 2014.

The line indicates the Sharpe Ratio associated with SPY. If an asset is above the line, it has a better risk-adjusted return than the S&P 500. Similarly, if as asset is below the line, the associated risk-adjusted return is poorer than SPY.

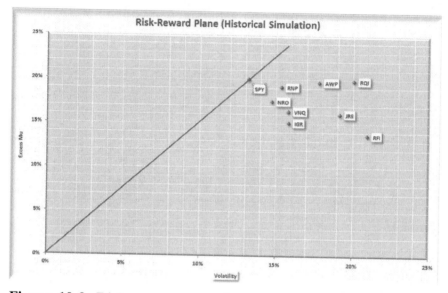

Figure 10-2. Risk versus reward over 3 years ending October, 2014

Some interesting observations can be gleamed from the figure.

- The S&P 500 easily outperformed REITs in terms of both absolute return and risk-adjusted return over the period of interest. This is not surprising since the S&P 500 was in a strong bull market. However, the chart is still valuable in that it shows relative performance among the different REIT funds.
- RNP and NRO had the best risk-adjusted performance of all the funds.
- VNQ (the ETF) had risk-adjusted performance in the middle of the pack.
- JRS and RFI lagged in performance over the period of analysis

- REIT funds were more volatile than the S&P 500
- Of the REIT funds, NRO and RNP had the lowest volatility.
- The funds RNP, NRO, VNQ, and IGR were tightly bunched in terms of risks. The other funds were more risky with RFI being the most risky over the period.

Summary

One of the reasons touted for owning REITs is the diversification they provide. In this regard, REIT lived up to their reputation and provided good diversification. REITs stocks often run hot or cold. Over the 3 years of the analysis, REITs did not outperform the general market but this could easily change in the future. I don't know when REITs will return to their glory days but if you are risk tolerant adding REITs to your portfolio is worthy of consideration.

Dr. John Dowdee

Chapter 11
Master Limited Partnership Funds

A Master Limited Partnership (MLP) is a partnership that is publicly traded. The MLP has two partners: a limited partner and a general partner. A limited partner is the person or group that provides the capital and receives periodic distributions from income. In a publicly traded company, this would typically be the shareholders (called unit holders in a partnership). The general partner is the person or group that actually manages the venture.

MLPs have relatively complex rules stemming from the Revenue Act of 1987, which provided tax advantages to partnerships that earn at least 90% of their income from "qualified" sources, primarily energy and natural resource activities. Most MLPs operate in the "midstream" portion of the energy production cycle, which involves the storing, transporting, or processing of energy (as opposed to "upstream" exploration or "downstream" retail sales). These MLPs typically have huge infrastructure expenditures, such as pipelines and processing plants. In terms of taxes, these infrastructure investments can be depreciated each year.

Over the last decade, Master Limited Partnerships (MLPs) have grown from a market cap of $30 billion to over $350 billion. An investor can purchase MLPs from his broker just like a regular stock. When you purchase these "stocks", you are actually purchasing a piece of a partnership rather than a piece of a corporation. So to be accurate, you are a unit holder rather than a stockholder. However, there is virtually no difference (except at tax reporting time) from purchasing units in a MLP than purchasing stock in a corporation. For convenience, we will refer to purchasing a unit as purchasing a stock.

Instead of purchasing an individual MLP stock, you can diversify your purchase by buying a fund that invests in MLP stocks. The funds come in all flavors including CEFs, ETFs, or ETNs. In addition to spreading your funds over many MLPs, one of the main benefits of using these funds is the simplification of tax reporting.

If you purchase a MLP stock, the income you receive from the stock is reported to the IRS using a relatively complex K-1 partnership form. The K-1 form is vastly different and much more complicated than the simple 1099 form for stock dividends. Although MLPs try to make filing a K-1 as easy as possible, it is still complex and confusing. To make matters worse, K-1 forms are not required to be issued until 15 March, much later than the January 31 date for 1099 forms. Thus, you may need to delay your tax filing until you receive all your K-1s. If you invest in MLP funds (CEFs, ETFs, or ETNs) you don't have to deal with K-1 forms; your distributions are reported on simple 1099 form, just like your other investments. This greatly simplifies tax reporting.

MLP CEFs

Some CEFs are structured as Registered Investment Companies (RICs). The good news is that RICs do not pay income taxes but instead pass on the tax liabilities to their shareholders. This is the structure used by most open-end mutual funds. The bad news is that RICs are prohibited from having more than 25% of their assets invested in MLPs. Thus, MLP CEFs that are structured as RICs are not pure MLP plays; they usually invest in subsidiaries and affiliates of MLPs, as well as other energy equities.

A more common structure for MLP CEFs is the C-corporation. These corporations can invest exclusively in MLPs but must pay corporate income tax. This may not be as detrimental as it sounds since the CEFs have ways to minimize these taxes. When a MLP pays out a distribution, the lion's share comes from depreciation allowances and is treated by the IRS as "return of capital". This "return of capital" serves to reduce the basis associated with the MLP purchase and taxes are not paid until the MLP is sold. So when a CEF receives a distribution from one of its constituent MLPs, the fund is able to write down the basis of the investment for the portion of the distribution. Over the years, the CEF often builds up relatively large amounts of deferred tax liability that will not be realized until the MLPs are sold. By IRS rules, these liabilities reduce the Net Asset Value (NAV). Astute investors recognize that the NAV has been "artificially" lowered, so these investors may be willing to pay a premium over the reported NAV.

I normally do not like to purchase CEFs selling at a large premium. However, for C-corporation MLP CEFs, some of the premium may be related to the decreased basis of MLPs rather than based purely on supply and demand. It is difficult to know exactly what percentage of the premium is tied to each phenomenon. Therefore, for C-corporation CEFs, I tend to compare the current premium to the "average premium" rather than using the absolute magnitude of the premium/discount. Current data on the average premium or discounts is available for free at http://www.cefconnect.com.

There are currently 26 MLP CEFs but many of these were launched after 2011 and do not have a long track record. Therefore, I will limit my analysis to funds that:

- Have at least a 3 year history
- That trade at least 50,000 shares per day
- Have a market cap of at least $200 million

The following 11 funds passed all my criteria.

Kayne Anderson Midstream Energy (KMF). This is a CEF structured as a RIC. The fund typically sells at a discount of between 5% and 9%. The portfolio consists of 100 holdings, 90% of which are invested in the midstream/energy sectors and consists of pure MLPs as well as MLP subsidiaries and affiliates. The fund uses 30% leverage and has an expense ratio of 3.9%, including interest expenses. The distribution is usually about 5% with no ROC.

Kayne Anderson Energy (KYE). This is a CEF structured as a RIC. The fund typically sells between a 5% discount and a premium of 2%. This fund has 96 holdings with 92% in MLP associated companies in the energy sector. The fund utilizes 29% leverage and has an expense ratio of 3.3%, including interest payment. The distribution is usually about 6% to 7% consisting of income, capital gains, and non-destructive ROC. This is one of the few MLP CEFs that has a history back to 2005 so we can obtain some sense of how MLPs performed in the 2008 bear market. In a word, KYE performed poorly, losing over 50% in 2008.

Kayne Anderson MLP (KYN). This CEF is structured as a C-corporation and typically sells for a premium between 4% and 8%. It holds about 70 MLP securities and uses 32% leverage. The expense ratio is 2.6% including interest. The distribution is usually about 6% consisting of income and non-destructive ROC. This fund also has a long history and lost over 50% of its NAV in 2008 (the price only declined 40%).

Kayne Anderson Energy Development (KED). This CEF is structured as a C-corporation and typically sells at a discount between 1% and 6%. The fund holds 55 securities, all MLPs and utilizes 22% leverage. The expense ratio is 3.8% and the distribution rate is usually about 5% to 6%, all from income with no ROC.

Fid/Claymore MLP Opportunity (FMO). This CEF is structured as a C-corporation and typically sells for a premium between 1% and 7%. This fund has about 50 holdings, all MLPs. It employs 23% leverage and has an expense ratio of 1.9% including interest payments. The distribution is usually about 6.0% consisting mostly of non-destructive return of capital. FMO performed relatively well in 2008, losing 35% in price and 46% in NAV.

ClearBridge Energy MLP (CEM). This CEF is structured as a C-corporation and typically sells between a discount of 2% and a premium of 2%. The portfolio has about 40 holdings, all of which are MLPs. The fund utilizes 21% leverage and has an expense ratio of 1.9%, including interest payments. The distribution is usually about 6%, which is mostly non-destructive return of capital.

ClearBridge Energy MLP Opportunities (EMO). This CEF is structured as a C-corporation and typically sells at a discount between 2% and 7%. The fund holds 45 MLPs and utilizes 21% leverage. The expense ratio is 2.3% including interest payments and the distribution rate is usually between 5% and 6%, most of which is non-destructive ROC.

Tortoise MLP Fund (NTG). This CEF is structured as a C-corporation and typically sells for a discount between 1% and 6%. The fund holds about 30 MLPs and uses leverage of 26%. The expense ratio is 1.5% and the distribution rate is usually about 6%, consisting mostly of non-destructive ROC.

Tortoise Energy Infrastructure (TYG). This CEF is structured as a C-corporation and typically sells at a premium between 1% and 10%. The fund holds about 30 MLPs and utilizes 25% leverage. The expense ratio is 1.7% and the distribution is around 5%, all from income with no ROC. During 2008, this fund lost 45% in both price and NAV.

Cushing MLP Total Return Fund (SRV). This CEF is structured as a C-corporation and typically sells for a whopping 19% to 20% premium. The fund holds about 55 securities with about 89% invested in MLPs. The fund uses 31% leverage and has an expense ratio of 2.2%. The distribution is a large, usually around 10% (which is likely the reason for the large premium), most of which is non-destructive ROC.

Nuveen Energy MLP Total Return (JMF). This CEF is structured as a C-corporation and typically sells at a discount between 1% and 7%. The fund holds 45 MLPs and utilizes 25% leverage. The expense ratio is 2% and the distribution rate is usually around 6%, consisting mostly of non-destructive ROC.

MLP ETFs/ETNs

There are currently about 3 MLP ETFs that are liquid (volume over 50,000 shares per day on average) with at least a 3 year history. These are summarized below.

ALPS Alerian MLP ETF (AMLP). This is an ETF that tracks the Alerian MLP Infrastructure Index, which consists of 25 pipeline and processing MLPs. This is one of the few ETFs tracking MLPs (most are structured as Exchange Traded Notes). AMPL is structured as a C-corporation to avoid the 25% limitation for MLP ownership. This has become one of the fastest growing exchange traded products, with an average daily volume of over 3 million shares. This ETF does not utilize leverage and has a low expense ratio of 0.85%. It has a yield of about 5.7%.

JPMorgan Alerian MLP Index (AMJ). This ETN tracks the Alerian MLP index, which consists of the 50 largest MLPs. An increased level of caution should be exercised if you plan to purchase

117

AMJ. In June, 2012 JP Morgan decided to cap the number of shares that were issued for AMJ. This was very unusual for an ETN and effectively changed the ETN into a closed-end product. With the number of shares fixed, the price is based on supply and demand and the ETN can sell at a premium. At the current time, AMJ is selling very near its NAV but it could deviate from the NAV in the future. The expense ratio is 0.85% and the yield is 4.8%.

UBS E-TRACS Alerian MLP Infrastructure (MLPI). This ETN tracks the Alerian MPL Infrastructure Index, which is a more concentrated portfolio of 25 pipeline and processing MLPs. It has an expense ratio of 0.85% and a yield of 4.7%.

Reference ETFs

SPY (the S&P 500 ETF) will be used for reference so we can compare the performance of MLPs with the general stock market.

Analysis of Candidates

Now that you have listed potential MLP funds for your portfolio, you need to check the correlation to see if they will provide a reasonable degree of diversification. As discussed in previous chapters, I do not like to select two assets if the correlation is above 80% since I would not receive adequate diversification.

Correlation

The correlations for the MLPs funds over a 3 year period (from October, 2011 to October, 2014) are shown in Figure 11-1. If the look-back period changes, then the correlations will also change but we have standardized on 3 years unless there is a compelling reason to look at other time frames.

	CEM	EMO	FMO	JMF	KED	KMF	KYE	KYN	NTG	SRV	TYG	AMJ	AMLP	MLPI	SPY
Correlation Matrix															
CEM	1.000														
EMO	0.638	1.000													
FMO	0.486	0.448	1.000												
JMF	0.622	0.610	0.493	1.000											
KED	0.447	0.454	0.409	0.511	1.000										
KMF	0.567	0.544	0.411	0.585	0.491	1.000									
KYE	0.586	0.515	0.415	0.563	0.532	0.650	1.000								
KYN	0.582	0.429	0.380	0.473	0.444	0.479	0.571	1.000							
NTG	0.541	0.523	0.487	0.520	0.425	0.524	0.495	0.402	1.000						
SRV	0.364	0.355	0.328	0.346	0.352	0.320	0.318	0.321	0.316	1.000					
TYG	0.403	0.394	0.350	0.431	0.301	0.420	0.409	0.363	0.420	0.230	1.000				
AMJ	0.606	0.565	0.446	0.606	0.489	0.555	0.546	0.526	0.554	0.343	0.433	1.000			
AMLP	0.570	0.541	0.436	0.591	0.449	0.522	0.502	0.558		0.310	0.442	0.860	1.000		
MLPI	0.594	0.559	0.437	0.588	0.473	0.528	0.548	0.582	0.544	0.333	0.448	0.877	0.929	1.000	
SPY	0.416	0.452	0.389	0.481	0.447	0.489	0.437	0.358	0.404	0.318	0.339	0.534	0.517	0.496	1.000

Figure 11-1 Correlation over 3 years

There are several observations from the correlation matrix.

- MLP CEFs are not highly correlated with the general market as represented by SPY. In fact, all the CEFs are less than 50% correlated with SPY.

- The three MLP ETFs (see bottom of matrix) are a little more correlated with SPY than the CEFs. However, the ETFs all have correlations less than 55%, which is excellent for diversification.

- Look at the right hand bottom of the matrix. This portion of the matrix portrays the correlations among the ETFs. These correction are very high, all over 87%. This indicates that you would not receive much diversification by buying multiple MLP ETFs.

- However, this conclusion does not apply to MLP CEFs. The correlations among CEFs are all less than 70% with most less than 60%. This implies that you can buy multiple MLP CEFs without worrying about losing diversification.

- You also receive diversification if you purchase MLP CEFs together with one MLP ETF. The correlations between the CEFs and ETFs are all small.

The conclusion is that MLPs offer excellent diversification for most portfolios and you will likely receive substantial diversification by adding these funds to a stock portfolio.

Risk versus Reward

The next step in our analysis is to plot the reward versus risk of each of these funds. This plot is shown in Figure 11-2 where the excess return (called Excess Mu) on the chart is plotted against volatility. This plot uses the same 3 year look-back period as the correlation matrix. The line shows the Sharpe Ratio associated with SPY. If an asset is above the line, it has a better risk-adjusted return than the S&P 500. Similarly, if as asset is below the line, the associated risk-adjusted return is poorer than SPY.

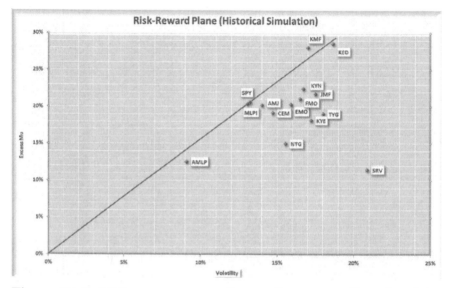

Figure 11-2. Risk versus reward over 3 years ending October, 2014

Some interesting observations are evident from the figure.

- As discussed previously, the S&P 500 was in a bull market during this period so few asset classes matched the performance of the general market. However, MLPI and KED had essentially the same risk-adjusted performance as SPY and KMF actually beat the S&P 500.
- AMPL was the least risky but also delivered the least return. However, on a risk-adjusted basis, AMLP was just below SPY in overall performance.
- KMF and KED had the highest absolute return but also had high volatility. Combining reward versus risk to determine

risk-adjusted performance, both of these CEFs had excellent results.

- The returns and volatilities of the majority of the ETFs and CEFs were bunched in the middle of the chart. The returns were for many of these funds was similar but the risks varied.
- The worst performer on a risk-adjusted basis was SRV and the best was KMF.
- There was not a significant trend in performance between CEFs structured as RICs and those structured as C-corporation. Of the two CEFs structured as RICs, KMF had excellent performance while KYE lagged most of the other CEFs.
- The CEF with the largest premium (SRV typically selling at a premium of over 20%) had the worst absolute and risk-adjusted performance. The volatility is increased by the large fluctuations in premium. Although this CEF provides the highest distribution, the risk-adjusted performance lagged the other CEFs.

Summary

The long term prospects for MLPs still appear to be bright. As the United States becomes more energy independent, there will be a growing demand for transporting oil, natural gas, and other fuels to their end-markets. This will result in a sweet spot for pipeline and mid-stream MLPs.

MLPs usually have large amounts of debt associated with maintaining their infrastructure, so higher interest rates present risks for this asset class. However, if interest rates remain low, as promised by the Fed, MLPs will be able to borrow cheaply, increasing their profits. On the other hand, if the economy falters and market sinks into another 2008 style bear markets, MLPs will not offer you protection.

No one knows what the future will hold but based on past performance, this asset class should be considered as a worthy addition to your portfolio.

Dr. John Dowdee

Chapter 12
Commodity and Agriculture Funds

Commodities are "real assets" that run the gamut from oil and precious metals to agriculture. Whether or not this volatile asset class deserves a place in a conservative portfolio is a matter of debate but many financial planners recommend from 3% to 10%, depending on your investment objectives, time horizons, and risk profile. There are two main reasons typically given for these recommendations. The first is that commodities provide a hedge against inflation since commodity prices tend to increase as the cost of living marches higher. The second reason is diversification. Commodities tend to have a low correlation with traditional asset such as stocks and bonds.

This chapter will consider two types of commodity funds: Agriculture focused funds and broad based commodity funds. The next chapter will consider precious metals. As you will see, over the last few years, commodities have not been in vogue and have not been good investments.

However, as documented in http://en.wikipedia.org/wiki/Commodity_price_shocks, over the years, commodities have had some sensational swings. Here are some examples:

- From 1971 to 1973, the price of corn and wheat increased by over 300%
- More recently in 2007 to 2008, the world experienced a food crisis that drove corn, wheat, and rice up by over 300% (but most prices collapsed as the world entered the 2008 bear market recession).
- The price of oil exploded to over $140 a barrel in 2007 only to sink in 2008

So commodities can be very lucrative when they are rising but they are definitely not "buy and forget" investments since prices can collapse as quickly as they rise. If you are a risk tolerant investor and want to at least consider this asset class, then please read the rest of this chapter.

Dr. John Dowdee

Feed your Portfolio with Agriculture Funds

Why invest in agriculture? Over the long term, prices for agricultural products will likely move higher because the increase in food production has not kept pace with population growth. Global population has doubled over the past 45 years and if the current 1.3% rate of growth persists, the world population will double again in 50 years. This is a lot of mouths to feed and there is virtually no more arable land or fresh water to spare. In addition, as the standard of living improves in emerging markets, people will consume more meat, which not only increases the demand for livestock but also decreases the supply of grain (about 5 to 6 pounds of grain is required to raise one pound of beef). New technology, such as improved fertilizer and genetically modified seeds, will help but demand is likely to outstrip supply forcing prices higher.

Over the shorter term, weather is the main driver, which can either facilitate a bountiful harvest or cause a crippling shortage. For example, in 2012, corn fell 40% after a record harvest while cocoa gained 21% because hot and dry weather in West Africa depressed production.

This section will analyze a few of the agricultural Exchange Traded Funds (ETFs) and Exchange Traded Notes (ETNs) to assess relative risk-adjusted performance over the past few years. Most agricultural products are perishable so it is not feasible to hold the product in storage for long periods. Thus, future contracts are typically used by funds to invest in grains and livestock. To aid in understanding these funds, I will review a few of the characteristics of futures. More details about future contracts were presented in Chapter 5.

Futures are contracts allowing you to buy a product at a fixed date in the future for an agreed upon price. Future contracts expire and if you want to maintain a position, you have to repurchase another future contract. Depending on market conditions, the longer dated future contract may sell at a higher price than the current contract so when the current contract nears expiration, it has to be rolled over to a more expensive contract. When this happens, you lose money even though the underlying index has not changed! This characteristic of rolling over to higher priced contracts is called "contango". Similarly, if the longer dated contract sells at lower price than the current contract, you will make money when you roll over the contract. This condition is called "backwardation". Historically, commodities are in contango about 70% of the time. The rolling methodology, called roll yield, is an important driver of overall fund performance.

ETFs hold these future contracts. However, some fund companies decided not to actually hold the contracts but instead promise to provide the same return you would receive from owning the futures. These agreements are called ETNs. Since the company issuing the ETN is obligated to pay the holder the same return (less fees) as would be obtained by investing in the underlying futures, the difference between ETFs and ETNs is small (assuming the fund company does not go bankrupt).

The number of agricultural ETFs/ETNs has expanded over the past few years and it is now possible to invest in a wide range of both individual and baskets of agricultural commodities. Unfortunately, many of these funds are small and illiquid and are not suitable for most investors. The ETFs/ETNs analyzed in this article were selected based on the following criteria:

- The fund must have adequate liquidity and trade an average of at least 40,000 shares per day.
- The fund must have at least $100 million market cap.
- The fund must invest exclusively in agricultural products.
- The fund must have at least 3 years of history.

The funds that satisfied these criteria are summarized below.

PowerShares DB Agriculture (DBA). This ETF tracks an index of 10 agricultural commodity futures. The composition of the portfolio is determined by a proprietary rule-based algorithm designed to obtain the best yield from rolling over future contracts. Currently, sugar is the largest component (13%) followed by live cattle, corn, soybeans, and cocoa. Some of the smaller constituents include coffee (9.5%), lean hogs (7.6%) and wheat (6.3%). The fund has an expense ratio of 0.85% and does not provide any yield.

ELEMENTS Rodgers International Commodity Agriculture (RJA). The ETF tracks the Rodgers International Commodity Index (RICI)-Agriculture Total Return Index, which contains 20 agricultural futures contracts. The largest components of the index are wheat (20%), corn (14%), cotton (12%) and soybeans (9%). The components in the index are reviewed and adjusted annually. The fund has an expense ratio of 0.75% and does not provide any yield.

iPath DJ-UBS Grains TR Sub-Index (JJG). This is an ETN that provides returns that are commensurate with the performance of unleveraged investments in grain future contracts. The index is composed of 41% corn, 37% soybeans, and 22% wheat. The fund has an expense ratio of 0.75% and does not provide any yield.

iPath DJ-UBS Coffee TR Sub-Index (JO). This is an ETN that provides returns that are commensurate with the performance of unleveraged investments in coffee future contracts. The fund has an expense ratio of 0.75% and does not provide any yield.

Teucrium Corn (CORN). This ETF tracks the price of corn futures by holding a portfolio of 3 separate corn future contracts (with expiration in different months). The use of separate contracts helps the fund manage roll. The fund has an expense ratio of 1.4% and does not provide any yield.

In addition to ETFs and ETNs that are based on futures, the following is an ETF that offers global exposure by investing in companies supporting the agriculture industry.

Market Vectors Agribusiness (MOO). This ETF holds 51 stocks that are associated with agriculture, including farming equipment, fertilizer, and seeds. The fund uses a modified cap weighting and the largest 10 holding make up almost 60% of the total assets. About half the portfolio is domiciled within the United States. The fund has an expense ratio of 0.55% and yields 1.9%.

Reference ETFs

SPY (the S&P 500 ETF) will be used for reference to compare the performance of agricultural funds with the general stock market.

Analysis of Candidates

Now that you have listed potential agricultural funds for your portfolio, you need to check the correlation to see if they will provide a reasonable degree of diversification. As usual, my criterion is to require correlations less than 80%.

Correlation Agriculture Funds

The correlations for the agricultural funds over a 3 year period (from October, 2011 to October, 2014) are shown in Figure 12-1. If the look-back period changes, then the correlations will also change but we have standardized on 3 years unless there is a compelling reason to look at other time frames.

Correlation Matrix	CORN	DBA	JJG	JO	MOO	RJA	SPY
CORN	1.000	0.66	0.88	0.12	0.16	0.78	0.09
DBA	0.658	1.000	0.73	0.59	0.33	0.82	0.22
JJG	0.877	0.726	1.000	0.14	0.20	0.91	0.13
JO	0.122	0.588	0.142	1.000	0.13	0.29	0.06
MOO	0.163	0.326	0.200	0.134	1.000	0.33	0.86
RJA	0.777	0.824	0.905	0.289	0.334	1.000	0.25
SPY	0.090	0.221	0.126	0.062	0.864	0.249	1.000

Figure 12-1 Correlation over 3 years

The correlation chart is very enlightening. The funds (either ETFs or ETNs) based on futures are virtually uncorrelated with the S&P 500. So these funds offer excellent diversification for an equity based portfolio. As you might expect, since MOO is based on stocks, it is highly correlated with SPY and does not offer adequate diversification.

If you wish to invest in more than one agricultural fund, then you need to review the pairwise correlations:

- CORN is highly correlated with JJG but provides good diversification relative to the other commodities.
- DBA is not highly correlated with any of the other funds except for RJA.
- JJG is highly correlated with RJA and CORN.
- JO provide excellent diversification with respect to the other commodities.
- RJA is highly correlated with DBA and JJG.

Reward versus Risk Agriculture Funds

Which fund should you choose? To gain insight, you can review the reward versus risk plot shown in Figure 12-2.

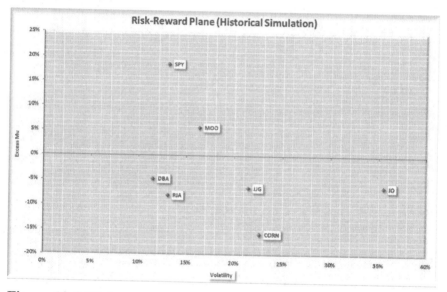

Figure 12-2 Risk versus reward past 3 years.

The figure indicates that over the past 3 years, the commodity funds have substantially underperformed the S&P 500. In fact, every fund, with the exception of MOO, has a negative return over the period so the Sharpe Ratio is not meaningful. However, you can still make some observations:

- The commodity funds were generally at least as risky as the S&P 500. DBA and RJA had about the same volatility as SPY but the rest of the funds were significantly more risky.
- Of all the commodities, coffee (JO) was the most risky.
- The more broad based agriculture funds (DBA and RJA) were less risky and lost less than most of the other funds.
- MOO has a positive return but is not a good portfolio candidate due to its high correlation with SPY coupled with the relative low return.

However, based on the risk versus reward plot, you would not want to choose any of these agricultural funds for your portfolio unless you expect the trend to change. If you think that the price of one or more of the commodities might be entering a bull market, then these funds would be worthy of consideration. But this volatile asset class is not for the fainthearted and I would recommend these funds only for the more risk tolerant investor.

Broad Based Commodity Funds

This section will analyze a few of the broad-based commodity ETFs and ETNs to assess relative risk-adjusted performance over the past three years. These broad based funds have a little of all the commodities including energy, precious metals, as well as agricultural goods.

The number of commodity ETFs/ETNs has expanded over the past few years and it is now possible to invest in a wide range of both individual and baskets of commodities. Unfortunately, many of these funds are small and illiquid and are not suitable for most investors. The ETFs/ETNs analyzed in this chapter are broad-based funds and were selected based on the following criteria:

- The fund must have adequate liquidity and trade an average of at least 30,000 shares per day.
- The fund must have a market cap of $100 million or more.
- The fund must invest exclusively in commodities.
- The fund must have at least 3 years of history.

The funds that satisfied these criteria are summarized below.

Dr. John Dowdee

PowerShares DB Commodity Index (DBC). This ETF tracks an index of 14 commodities from four sectors. Energy makes up 55% of the portfolio and includes oil, gasoline, and heating oil futures. The second highest allocation is agriculture at 22% and includes sugar, corn, wheat, and soybean futures. Industrial metals consume 13% of the portfolio and includes copper, zinc, and aluminum. Precious metals weigh in at 10% and includes gold and silver futures. The fund utilizes a roll strategy that tries to optimize the roll yield. The fund has an expense ratio of 0.85% and does not provide any yield.

iPath DJ UBS Commodity Index (DJP). This is an ETN that promises to pay holders the same return as a broad-based index of 20 commodities. Agriculture (grains) and energy each make up about a third of the portfolio. The remaining third is split among industrial metals, precious metals, and livestock. This ETN employs a roll strategy based on the rolling the front month, which makes it susceptible to contango. The ETN has an expense ratio of 0.75% and does not provide any yield.

iShares S&P GSCI Commodity-Indexed Trust (GSG). This ETF is heavily weighted (70%) toward energy (oil, natural gas, and gasoline). The rest of the portfolio is split among agriculture (15%). industrial metals (7%), livestock (5%) and precious metals (3%). The fund employs a roll strategy based on rolling the front month, which makes it susceptible to contango. The fund has an expense ratio of 0.75% and does not provide any yield.

UBS E-TRACS CMCI Total Return (UCI). This ETN tracks a basket of 26 commodity futures over different maturity dates from 3 months to 3 years. The portfolio is comprised of 34% energy, 27% industrial metals, 5% precious metals, 30% agriculture, and 4% livestock. UCI is not very liquid so you should use only limit orders if you decide to buy or sell this fund. The fund has an expense ratio of 0.65% and does not provide any yield.

ELEMENTS Rodgers International Commodity (RJI). This ETN tracks an index of 37 commodity future contracts, making it one of the most diversified baskets of commodities. It is rebalanced monthly based on worldwide consumption. Typically, energy makes up about 44% of the index, metals weigh in at 21%, and agriculture is 32%. The fund's return is based on rolling over future contracts each month so

130

it may experience contango, depending on market conditions. The fund has an expense ratio of 0.75% and does not provide any yield.

GreenHaven Continuous Commodity Index (GCC). This ETF tracks 17 equally weighted commodity futures. The equal weighting translates to more emphasis on agricultural products (46%) and less focus on energy (18%) than its peers. Other holding include 24% allocated to metals and 12% to livestock. To mitigate contango, this fund purchases a set of future contracts covering a six month period rather than just the front month. The fund has an expense ratio of 0.85% and does not provide any yield.

United States Commodity Index (USCI). This ETF tracks an index using a rule based methodology to select 14 commodities out of a pool of 27. The selection is based on contango and momentum and the selected futures are weighted equally for the month. The portfolio changes each month but over a long period, energy has averaged about 25% of the portfolio with grains coming in second at 22%. The fund was launched in 2010 so does not have a long history. It has an expense ratio of 0.95% and does not provide any yield.

Analysis of Candidates (Broad Based Funds)

Now that you have listed potential commodity funds for your portfolio, you need to check the correlation to see if they will provide a reasonable degree of diversification.

Correlation (Broad Based Funds)

The correlations for the commodity funds over a 3 year period (from October, 2011 to October, 2014) are shown in Figure 12-3.

	DBC	DJP	GCC	GSG	RJI	UCI	USCI	SPY
DBC	1.000	0.90	0.84	0.94	0.95	0.81	0.87	0.50
DJP	0.898	1.000	0.92	0.81	0.91	0.80	0.88	0.41
GCC	0.835	0.918	1.000	0.74	0.86	0.75	0.85	0.43
GSG	0.942	0.814	0.740	1.000	0.92	0.77	0.80	0.48
RJI	0.949	0.908	0.860	0.921	1.000	0.81	0.87	0.50
UCI	0.815	0.799	0.749	0.767	0.815	1.000	0.75	0.43
USCI	0.866	0.876	0.854	0.802	0.868	0.748	1.000	0.47
SPY	0.499	0.413	0.429	0.480	0.499	0.425	0.471	1.000

Correlation Matrix

Figure 12-3 Correlation over 3 years

The correlation chart is very interesting. As you can easily see, commodity funds do offer excellent diversification with respect to the general stock market. However, generally, the commodity funds are highly correlated with one another (there are only a couple of funds with correlations less than 80%). Therefore, if I wanted to have commodity exposure, I would only purchase one fund (rather than multiple funds).

Reward versus Risk (Broad Based Funds)

Which fund should you choose? To gain insight, you can review the reward versus risk plot shown in Figure 12-4.

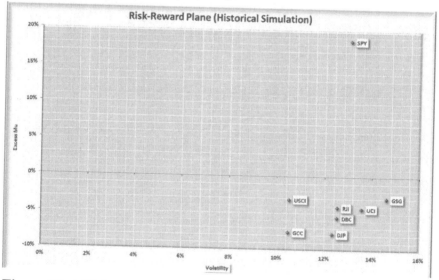

Figure 12-4 Risk versus Reward past 3 years Commodities

The figure indicates that over the past 3 years, the commodity funds have substantially underperformed the S&P 500. In fact, every fund has a negative return over the period so the Sharpe Ratio is not meaningful. However, you can still make some observations:

- The commodity funds have roughly the same risk as the overall stock market with GSG exhibiting the highest risk and USCI and GCC being the least risky.
- From the chart, you can infer that USCI had the best performance since it had the least negative return along with the least risk.

However, you would not want to choose any of these commodity funds for your portfolio unless you expect the trend to change. Figure 12-3 is a plot of the price of RJI from its inception in 2007 to October 2014 (the time this chapter was written). I chose RJI since it is diversified and is a good proxy for the commodity market. After peaking in 2007, commodities nosedived in 2008 (along with just about every other asset). However, unlike stocks, commodities ran out of steam in 2011 and have been flat to down ever since.

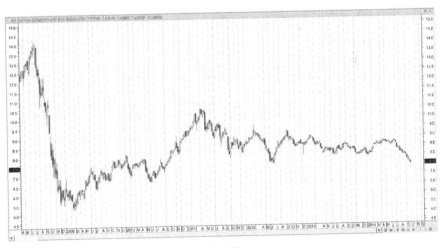

Figure 12-5 Plot of the price of RJI

Summary

Commodity funds do provide reasonable diversification for a general equity portfolio so are worthy of consideration but they have not been a rewarding asset class, especially over the past 3 years. If inflation picks up, the performance of commodities should improve. However, since inflation has been dormant since these funds were launched, it has not been possible to confirm or deny the inflation protection afforded by this asset class. If you are a risk tolerant investor and would like to delve into broad based commodities, I would recommend taking a look at USCI and RJI as candidates for your portfolio.

Chapter 13
Gold and Precious Metals Funds

Gold bullion has had an illustrious and volatile past. In 1934, a year after the U.S. went off the gold standard, the price of gold was pegged by the government at $35 per ounce. It stayed at this value until 1971 when President Nixon allowed the value to float. And float it did, hitting a high of $850 an ounce in 1980. It subsequently collapsed to $250 an ounce in the late 1980s and stayed in a relatively narrow trading range for the next decade. During the early years of the new millennium, gold blasted off, reaching a price of over $1900 in late 2011. Many called this a "bubble" but it is interesting to note that the gold's peak price of $850 in 1980 is equivalent to an inflation adjusted price of over $2,300 today. After reaching the 2011 peak, the infatuation with gold died and gold entered bear market territory, dropping to below $1,200 an ounce in 2014.

There is no doubt that gold and other precious metals are volatile assets. Whether or not they deserve a place in a retirement portfolio is a matter of debate. Some pundits, like Alexander Green, who formulated the "Gone Fishing Portfolio" recommends about 5%. Others, like Harry Browne, in his "Permanent Portfolio" believes as much as 25% is justified. Still others, like Bill Schultheis' "Coffee House Portfolio" does not allocate any to precious metals. There is, of course, no right answer. It depends on your investment objectives, time horizons, and risk profile. This book does not try to justify any percentage allocation to precious metals. However, if you decide to include them in your portfolio, then this section will provide an analysis of how the different types of precious metal securities have performed on a risk-adjusted basis.

There are a number of ETFs and CEFs that focus on gold and silver. For this analysis, I chose representatives that had at least a three year history and were liquid (trading at least 30,000 shares on average per day). These selections are summarized below.

SPDR Gold Shares (GLD). One share of this ETF represents a tenth of an ounce of gold. It is not the cheapest (expense ratio of 0.4%) but is by far the most liquid, trading more than 6 million shares per day on average. The bullion backing this ETF is held in vaults in London. Gains from this ETF are taxed like you owned the physical gold directly (taxed at collectibles rate if you hold for more than a year). Note that other gold bullion ETFs like **iShares Gold Trust (IAU)** and **PowerShares DB Gold ETF (DGL)**, are highly correlated (99%) with GLD and were not included in the analysis.

Sprott Physical Gold Trust (PHYS). This is a CEF with an inception date of February, 2010. This fund holds only gold bullion so is highly correlated (97%) with GLD. Because of the high correlation, I have not included PHYS in the analysis but I am summarizing it here because it has a unique marketing feature. This fund allows you to receive gold bullion in lieu of cash if you decide to redeem the fund. Before you rush out and buy, make sure you read the fine print. The redemption in bullion is only available in multiples of gold bars. Since a gold bar weighs between 350 and 450 ounces, this is a minimum of more than $400,000 even at 2014's low gold prices; plus you would also have to pay for an armored car for the delivery. So I don't think many people will take advantage of the gold redemption option. However, the idea was brilliant and likely was one of the factors in generating over a 20% premium in 2010. But like all the other gold CEFs, the shares now sell at or below their Net Asset Value (NAV). The fund continues to have great liquidity, with a volume exceeding a half million shares daily.

Central Gold Trust (GTU). This CEF seeks to replicate the performance of gold bullion. It holds gold bullion at the Canadian Imperial Bank of Commerce and does not lease gold. One of the main differences between GTU and GLD is that GTU is a CEF, which can sell at a premium or discount. Currently, this fund is selling at a 10% discount! During past bull markets, this fund has sold for a 10% premium so the price of the fund fluctuates more than GLD, but there also is the potential of higher returns. This fund does not use leverage and has an expense ratio of 0.4%. It does not pay any distribution. As you might expect, this CEF is highly correlated (93%) with GLD so will not be included in the analysis. However, it is presented here as an alternative to GLD.

iShares Silver Trust (SLV). One share of this ETF tracks the price of one ounce of silver bullion. The shares are backed by silver held in banks in London and New York. Silver is more volatile than gold, primarily because it is sensitive to industrial demand in addition to being a "safe haven" asset. This is not all bad since the industrial uses may serve to support prices if the desire for silver wanes among investors. This fund is very liquid (average 7 million shares per day) and has an expense ratio of 0.5%, which is similar to other funds. Like GLD, gains from SLV are taxed as collectibles.

Central Fund of Canada (CEF). This is a closed end fund that holds roughly 50% gold bullion and 50% silver bullion. As a closed end fund, it can sell at a premium or discount to Net Asset Value (NAV). During the heyday of the precious metal frenzy, the fund sold at a 15% premium. Over the past 3 years, it has averaged selling between a small premium and a 5% discount but occasionally the discount will deepen. This fund does not use leverage and has a low expense ratio of 0.3%. It is relatively liquid for a closed end fund, trading about a million shares per day. For tax purposes, this fund is a passive foreign investment company so you should consult your tax advisor relative to the treatment of gains and losses.

Market Vector Gold Miners (GDX). This ETF holds 30 cap-weighted precious metal mining companies (mostly gold miners but with a few silver miners). The three largest holdings are Goldcorp (GG), Barrick Gold (ABX), and Newmont Mining (NEM). A little over 60% of the assets are Canadian companies with the rest primarily in the US and South Africa. It is extremely liquid (over 40 million shares per day) and has a reasonable expense ratio of 0.5%.

Market Vector Junior Gold Miners (GDXJ). This ETF is a rule based fund that provides investors with exposure to small cap companies in the gold and silver mining industry. It holds 63 junior gold and silver miners. Most of the miners (75%) are domiciled in North America but about 21% are Asian mines. It has an expense ratio of 0.57% and does not provide any yield.

GAMCO Global Gold Natural Resources and Income (GGN). This CEF writes options on gold and natural resources stocks. The fund typically sells between a small 1% discount and a 2% premium. It has 110 holding, primarily precious metal companies but some oil and other resource stocks. About 75% of the holdings are from North American firms. It uses a small amount of leverage (8%) and has an expense ratio of 1.3%. It usually has a large distribution of about 11% to 12% but a large percentage of this may be return of capital (ROC). The ROC may be destructive when natural resources are in a bear market.

GAMCO Natural Resources Gold and Income (GNT). This CEF is a sister fund to GGN. It also writes options on gold and natural resource stocks and typically sells between small premiums and a discount of 4%. The fund holds about 95 gold miners and other resource stocks. The fund does not use leverage and has an expense ratio of 1.2%. The distribution is usually around 11% but a large percentage may be ROC and may be destructive if the portfolio is not appreciating.

ASA Gold and Precious Metal (ASA). This CEF typically sells at a discount between 6% and 8%. It is a concentrated fund with only about 40 precious metal mining companies. About 45% of the miners are Canadian with the rest spread primarily among the United States, South Africa, the Channel Islands, and Australia. The fund does not use leverage and has an expense ratio of 0.8%. It has a small distribution of 1.4%, paid from income with no ROC.

ETFS Physical Platinum (PPLT). Platinum is used primarily in industrial applications and jewelry, rather than being held as a hedge against fiat currency. It is rarer than gold and the price is usually, but not always, higher than gold. A primary use of platinum is in automobile catalytic converters but it also has a wide demand in jewelry, especially when the price falls below gold. One share of PPLT represents about a tenth of an ounce of platinum. It is not nearly as liquid as other precious metal ETFs (trading only about 60,000 shares per day). The ETF holds bullion in banks in London and Zurich. Like the other precious metal ETFs, gains are taxed as collectibles. The fund has an expense ratio of 0.65%.

ETFS Physical Palladium (PALL). Palladium is a lesser known precious metal that sells for about $725 per ounce. In can be used instead of platinum in catalytic converters and in jewelry. It has many of the same properties as other precious metals in that it is malleable, easy to polish and remains tarnish free. In Europe, 15% palladium is typically alloyed with gold to produce "white gold". Palladium is used primarily for industrial applications and is generally not considered a "safe haven" asset. Each share of PALL represents about a tenth of an ounce of Palladium. The ETF trades over 100,000 shares per day so it is relatively liquid. The bullion associated with the ETF is stored in vaults in London and Zurich. The fund has an expense ratio of 0.6%. Like gold and silver, it is taxed like collectibles.

Sprott Physical Platinum and Palladium (SPPP). This CEF is a new kid on the block (launched December, 2012). Because of the short history, it will not be included in the analysis. However, it is summarized here because of its unique portfolio consisting of equal dollar amount of both platinum and palladium. This fund typically sells near the NAV and has an expense ratio of 0.35%. It does not provide any distributions.

Global X Silver Miners (SIL). This ETF holds 31 cap-weighted silver mining companies, of which Silver Wheaton (SLW) is the largest holding. Almost 95% of the constituents are based in either North America or Latin America. It is relatively liquid (trading about 200,000 shares per day) and has an expense ratio of 0.65%.

Reference ETFs
As usual, we will use the SPY (the S&P 500 ETF) for reference

Analysis of Candidates

Now that you have listed potential precious metal funds for your portfolio, you need to check the correlation to see if they will provide a reasonable degree of diversification. As discussed in previous chapters, I do not like to select two assets if the correlation is above 80%.

Correlation Precious Metal

The correlations for the precious metal funds over a 3 year period (from October, 2011 to October, 2014) are shown in Figure 13-1.

Correlation Matrix

	ASA	CEF	GDX	GDXJ	GGN	GLD	GNT	PALL	PPLT	SIL	SLV	SPY
ASA	1.000											
CEF	0.715	1.000										
GDX	0.893	0.755	1.000									
GDXJ	0.850	0.745	0.904	1.000								
GGN	0.647	0.598	0.633	0.622	1.000							
GLD	0.720	0.912	0.767	0.756	0.592	1.000						
GNT	0.655	0.567	0.635	0.634	0.791	0.557	1.000					
PALL	0.425	0.544	0.435	0.452	0.424	0.541	0.461	1.000				
PPLT	0.585	0.696	0.603	0.601	0.513	0.724	0.542	0.725	1.000			
SIL	0.870	0.785	0.921	0.896	0.696	0.774	0.714	0.507	0.652	1.000		
SLV	0.675	0.916	0.720	0.705	0.576	0.867	0.554	0.576	0.707	0.776	1.000	
SPY	0.317	0.221	0.290	0.317	0.413	0.191	0.518	0.402	0.354	0.421	0.307	1.000

Figure 13-1 Correlation of precious metal funds over 3 years

There are several observations from the correlation matrix.

- The funds (either ETFs or CEFs) have low correlations with the S&P 500. So these funds do offer excellent diversification for an equity based portfolio.
- As expected, among the funds, some are correlated with each other while others are relatively uncorrelated.
- Gold stocks are correlated with the associated metal but not as much as you might think. For example, gold miners (GDX and GDXJ) are only 76% correlated with the price of gold (GLD).
- Similar to gold, silver stocks (SIL) are only moderately correlated (77%) with the price of silver (SLV).
- Funds that hold bullion are highly correlated with one another. For example, CEF is highly correlated (91%) with the price of gold (GLD) and the price of silver (SLV).
- Palladium (PALL) and platinum (PPLT) are not highly correlated with the other precious metals.

Reward versus Risk Precious Metals

If you decide to have some precious metal in your portfolio, which fund should you choose? To gain insight, you can review the reward versus risk plot shown in Figure 13-2.

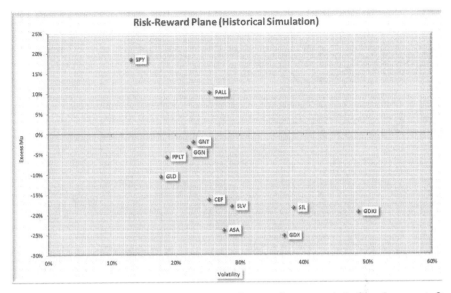

Figure 13-2: Risk versus reward precious metal funds past 3 years.

The figure indicates that over the past 3 years, precious metals have substantially underperformed the S&P 500. In fact, every fund, with the exception of Palladium (PALL), has a negative return over the period so the Sharpe Ratio is not meaningful. However, you can still make some observations:

- Precious metal funds are more volatile than the S&P 500.
- There is a wide range of risks associated with precious metals. The bullion funds (GLD, SLV, PPLT, PALL, and CEF) are more volatile than the associated stock funds. However, writing options (GNT, GNN) tends to dampen the volatility.
- Silver is more volatile than gold.
- As you might expect, the junior gold stock fund is by far the most volatile.
- Over the past 3 years, palladium was the best performing precious metal. The other funds losing the least were GNT, GGN, PPLT, and GLD.

Based on the risk versus reward plot, you would not want to choose any of these precious metal funds for your portfolio unless you expect the trend to change. Figure 13-3 is a plot of the price of GLD. As shown on the chart, GLD went from about $40 per share (Gold bullion at about $400 per ounce) in 2004 to over $185 per share (Gold price over $1850 per ounce) in 2011. Since 2011 gold bullion has been in a steep correction, falling back down to about $1150 per ounce. So gold can be a great asset in your portfolio but you must be careful.

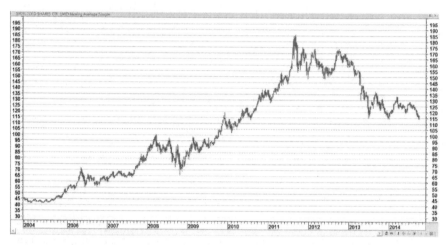

Figure 13-3 Gold prices since 2004

Summary Precious Metal Funds

Precious metal funds do provide excellent diversification for a general equity portfolio so are worthy of consideration but this has not been a rewarding asset class, especially over the past 3 years. If you are a risk tolerant investor and expect the precious metals to return to their glory years, then you might want to take a look at these funds for possible inclusion in your portfolio.

Chapter 14
Currency ETFs

The currency market (called the foreign exchange, Forex, or the FX market) is the largest and most liquid market in the world. The volume of FX trading is over 3 trillion dollars per day, which is an order of magnitude greater than the trading volume on all the world's stock exchanges combined. In the past, it was difficult for retail investors to gain access to this market since you needed an account with a forex broker. All this changed in 2005 when Rydex Investments launched the first currency Exchange Traded Fund (ETF) based on the value of the euro. Now there are over 29 currency ETFs and one currency Closed End Fund (CEF).

Most retail investors are not be familiar with the characteristics of currency funds so this chapter will present a quick tutorial. The primary reason for the FX market is to facilitate the exchange of one currency into another by multi-national corporations. On a much smaller scale, everyone who has traveled abroad is familiar with foreign exchange rates. If you travel to Europe, you will need to convert your dollars to euros at the current rate (at the time of this writing) of 0.72 euros per dollars. So if you buy a product for 72 euros it will cost you $100 in terms of dollars. This rate is not fixed. For example, in 2010 the dollars was worth .80 euros so the same 72 euro product would have cost only $90 dollars. This was because the dollar was "stronger" in 2010 than it is today.

The above illustrates that currencies are traded as pairs based on the price of one currency in terms of another. The seven most liquid pairs are (where the word "Dollar" without a qualifier refers to the U.S. dollar):

- Euro/ Dollar
- Dollar/Japanese Yen
- British Pound/Dollar
- Dollar/Swiss Franc
- Australian Dollar/Dollar
- Dollar/Canadian Dollar

- New Zealand Dollar/Dollar

Some other aspects of the currency market are:

- Trading currencies is a zero-sum game as opposed to trading stocks, which have a long term positive expectation. If one currency appreciates, another currency must depreciate.
- The forex market is open from the start of the business day on Monday in the Asia-Pacific time zone to the Friday close of business in New York.
- Currencies are not traded on an exchange and trading is not controlled by a clearing house or a central governing body.
- There are no commissions. Brokers make money on the spread between the buying and selling price.
- There are no limits on the amount of currency you can buy. If you wanted to buy $1 billion U.S. dollars, the transaction could be easily accommodated.
- The value of a currency is established by supply and demand. Some factors influencing the demand include interest rates, inflation, and stability of the economy. The supply can be affected if governments intervene in the market to buy or sell huge quantities of currency. For example, if Japan wants to increase the popularity of their exports, the government may want to weaken the yen, which will make Japanese goods more attractive to foreign buyers. This could lead to "currency wars" where governments jockey for position in the international trade markets. These political interventions may result in unnatural fluctuations in the market.
- The currency "carry trade" is a strategy where the investor sells a currency with a low interest rate and buys a currency with a higher interest rate. The investor tries to profit from the difference between the two rates.

To limit the number of funds I included in my analysis, I did not include any inverse or bear funds and required the funds to meet the following criteria:

- Have at least a 3 year history
- Trade at least an average of 50,000 shares per day
- Have a market cap of at least $150 million.

The ETFs and CEFs described below passed my screen.

PowerShares DB US Dollar Index Bullish (UUP). This ETF tracks the U.S. dollar against a basket of currencies consisting of the euro, Japanese yen, British pound, Canadian dollar, Swedish krona, and the Swiss franc. The euro is weighted at 58%, the Japanese yen at 14%, and the British pound at 12%. The other currencies make up the remaining 16%. The fund uses future contracts to maintain the currency exposure. UUP is structured as a limited partnership so investors will receive a K-1 form at the end of the year rather than a 1099 form. The fund does not pay any dividends and the expense ratio of 0.75%.

PowerShares DB G10 Currency Harvest (DBV). This EFT implements a "carry trade" strategy using a quantitative algorithm for buying and selling future contracts. This makes a sophisticated "hedge-fund" technique available to individual investors with a tiny fraction of the fees charged by hedge funds. The fund can select from any currency used by the following countries: United States, Canada, Japan, Australia, New Zealand, Great Britain, Switzerland, Euro Zone, Norway, or Sweden. The fund utilizes 2 times leverage and buys higher yielding currencies while shorting the lower yielding currencies. Because this fund uses future contracts and is structured as a limited partnership, it has some unique tax consequences that should be discussed with your tax advisor. The fund does not pay any dividends and has an expense ratio of 0.81%.

CurrencyShares Australian Dollar Trust (FXA). The Currency Shares funds are managed by Guggenheim Investments who purchased Rydex in 2010. FXA is an ETF designed to track the price of the Australian dollar. It is organized as an exchange traded grantor trust, which means that the fund invests in a static basket of Australian dollars. Each share of the fund represents a fractional interest in this portfolio of Australian dollars. The fund yields 2% and has an expense ratio of 0.40%.

CurrencyShares Canadian Dollar Trust (FXC). This ETF is designed to track the price of the Canadian dollar. Similar to FXA, this fund is also organized as a grantor trust that invests in Canadian dollars. The fund yields 0.2% and has an expense ratio of 0.40%.

CurrencyShares Euro Trust (FXE). This ETF is designed to track the price of the euro. It is a grantor trust that invests in the euro. It does not generate any yield and has an expense ratio of 0.40%.

CurrencyShares Japanese Yen Trust (FXY). This ETF is designed to track the price of the Japanese yen. It is a grantor trust that invests in the yen. It does not generate any yield and has an expense ratio of 0.40%.

WisdomTree Chinese Yuan Strategy (CYB). This ETF seeks to achieve a total return associated with the interest rate in China and changes in value of the Chinese yuan. Since the money markets associated with Chinese securities are not very liquid, the fund employs a sophisticated strategy based on forward contracts and currency swaps to achieve its objectives. The fund is short term oriented, generally having a portfolio maturity of 90 days or less for money market instruments and a maturity of 6 months or less for forward contracts. The fund yields 0.8% and has an expense ratio of 0.45%.

Nuveen Diversified Currency Opportunity (JGT). The CEF typically sells at a discount between 11% and 13%. The fund's objective is to seek current income and total return by investing in short duration global bonds, forward currency contracts, and other derivatives. The portfolio consists of about 60% foreign government bonds denominated in local currency, 11% invested in foreign government bonds denominated in U.S. dollars, 9% in investment grade corporate bonds, 7% in U.S treasuries, and 6% in high yield bonds. In terms of geographic distribution, 20% of the assets are from the U.S, 15% from Brazil, 13% from Canada, 12% from Mexico, and the rest from other countries. The fund does not use leverage and has an expense ratio of 1%. The distribution is about 7%, funded from income, gains, and return of capital.

Reference ETFs

In previous chapters, we have used the S&P 500 as the reference for comparative performance. However, you would not expect currencies to behave like stocks. You will likely invest in currencies as an alternative to bonds. Therefore, in addition to SPY, I used the **iShares**

7-10 tear Treasury Bond (IEF) ETF as a reference. This ETF tracks the Barclay U.S. 7-10 Year Treasury Bond index, yields 1.75%, and has an expense ratio of 0.15%.

Analysis of Candidates

Now that you have a list of currency funds, you need to check the correlation to see if they will provide a reasonable degree of diversification. As discussed in previous chapters, I do not like to select two assets if the correlation is above 80%. Any correlations lower than 80% are fine but the lower the better.

Correlation Currency Funds

The correlations for currency funds over a 3 year period (from October, 2011 to October, 2014) are shown in Figure 14-1.

Correlation Matrix

	CYB	DBV	FXA	FXC	FXE	FXY	JGT	UUP	IEF	SPY
CYB	1.000	0.17	0.24	0.19	0.19	0.00	0.15	-0.20	-0.06	0.13
DBV	0.174	1.000	0.23	0.51	0.23	-0.28	0.37	-0.22	-0.12	0.57
FXA	0.241	0.726	1.000	0.65	0.51	0.21	0.29	-0.58	-0.15	0.54
FXC	0.190	0.510	0.655	1.000	0.49	0.15	0.29	-0.58	-0.10	0.41
FXE	0.185	0.228	0.511	0.490	1.000	0.17	0.22	-0.56	-0.10	0.22
FXY	0.004	-0.280	0.209	0.150	0.172	1.000	-0.04	-0.37	0.43	0.22
JGT	0.152	0.372	0.350	0.289	0.221	-0.044	1.000	-0.24	-0.06	0.39
UUP	-0.198	-0.223	-0.585	-0.580	-0.957	-0.374	-0.237	1.000	0.01	0.45
IEF	-0.058	-0.304	-0.121	-0.153	-0.105	0.427	-0.061	0.012	1.000	0.45
SPY	0.129	0.623	0.571	0.544	0.411	-0.219	0.452	-0.390	-0.450	1.000

Figure 14-1 Correlation currency funds over 3 years

There are several observations from the correlation matrix.

- UUP tracks the dollar against a basket of currencies. The only way the dollar can increase in value is if some of the other currencies decrease. Thus, UUP is negatively correlated with the other currencies.
- More interesting is the fact that intermediate terms bonds are negatively correlated with most currencies except for the U.S. dollar and the Japanese yen. A negative correlation is a "hedge". For example, if you own IEF and believe that it may

go down in price but do not want to sell it due to tax reasons, you can hedge against the anticipated decline by buying currency funds, such as DBV. If IEF does decrease as anticipated, the currency funds should appreciated, thus offsetting some of your losses. Hedging is a valuable technique and will be discussed in more detail in the sequel to this book providing strategies for risk management.

- The stock market is also negatively correlated with the UUP. Thus, if the dollar increases in value, the stock market will have a tendency to move lower (likely because international firms make less money if the dollar is strong).
- Currencies definitely provide diversification for a general market portfolio. All the currency funds have a low correlation with SPY and as discussed above, UUP provides a hedge (negative correlation) with respect to SPY.
- Currency funds are generally not correlated with each other since currencies seldom move in sync with one another. Thus, you will continue to receive diversification if you purchase multiple currency funds (but you have to be careful to decide if you want to diversify or hedge since you can achieve either objective with currencies).

Reward versus Risk Currency Funds

If currency funds intrigue you, the next step is to determine if they have been good investments in the past. To gain insight, you can review the reward versus risk plot shown in Figure 14-2.

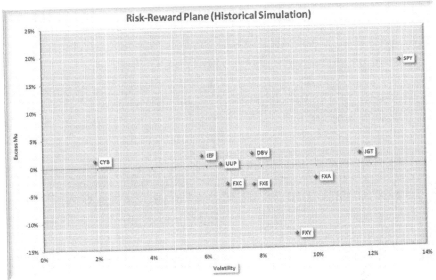

Figure 14-2: Risk versus reward currency funds for past 3 years.

As with commodities and precious metals, currencies have not been a good investment over the recent past. None of these funds come close to SPY in either absolute performance or risk-adjusted performance. As the plot illustrates, many of the funds have produced negative returns over the past 3 years. Even though the Sharpe Ratio is not a good metric when dealing with negative returns, some observations can still be made.

- Currencies are not as volatile as the stock market. The Chinese Yuan is very stable since its value is controlled by the Chinese government. However, even the free market currencies have relative small volatilities.

- In general, intermediate Treasury bonds, as exemplified by IEF, had a significantly better risk-adjusted performance than the vast majority of currency funds. Currencies are also generally more volatile than the intermediate Treasury Bonds.

- With the exception of the Japanese yen, which has performed horribly in the recent past, most currency fund prices are relatively stable. Most countries try to keep their currency in a relatively small range so you would not expect to either gain or lose a significant amount from these currency funds.

Dr. John Dowdee

Summary Currency Funds

Currency ETFs provide a simple and easy way to benefit from changes in the value of currencies without resorting to forex accounts. In particular, they provide investors with non-correlated assets to facilitate diversifying a stock market portfolio. However, with a few exceptions, over the past 3 years, currency ETFs have not provided rewards that were commensurate with risks.

No one knows what the future will hold but in the past, the diversification you might receive from investing in currency funds did not compensate for the potential dismal performance. Based on this data, I would be wary of adding currency funds to my portfolio unless the trend changes.

Part III
How to Construct a Sleep Soundly Portfolio

Chapter 15. Sleep Soundly CEF Portfolio

Chapter 16. Sleep Soundly ETF Portfolio

Chapter 17. Parting Thought

Important Notice

To fit the requirements of this book, the figures had to be reduced in size and printed in black and white. To view the charts in full size and in color, please go to www.SuperchargeRetirementIncome.com and click on Book Charts or follow the link below

http://superchargeretirementincome.com/02/knowledge-center/supercharge-retirement-income-charts-for-book/

Dr. John Dowdee

Chapter 15

Constructing a Sleep Soundly Portfolio with CEFs

This chapter will use the ideas presented in the previous chapters to construct a portfolio that will allow you to sleep soundly at night. This defensive portfolio is less volatile than the general stock market (S&P 500) but still delivers adequate returns. I will use closed end funds in this example because they are actively managed and offer excellent distributions.

Please note that I am not suggesting that this portfolio is right for everyone. It should be used as an example rather than an actionable recommendation. By the time you read this, the market may be very different from it was in early October, 2014 when this was written. However, by using the techniques presented here you can construct your own unique portfolio that is right for you and also right for the prevailing market conditions. With these caveats in mind, let's go about constructing a Sleep Soundly portfolio

First off, the market since 2009 has been on a tear, rising about 300%. It is now the 4th longest bull market since the Great Depression. I have no idea what the future may hold but as a retiree, I am beginning to worry. I do not have time to recoup from devastating losses like many suffered in the 2008 bear market. Thus, even though I may limit my potential upside, I have decided to move my portfolio into a more defensive position that will allow me to "sleep soundly" each night. Based on these considerations, I decided to construct a portfolio that contained about 50% equities and 50% bonds. In addition, I wanted to diversify within the equity and bond sectors. Therefore, I decided on the following mix:

Example Equity Portfolio
For the equity portion, I wanted to select representatives from the following asset classes:

- General equity
- Preferred stocks

- Real Estate Investment Trusts (REITS)
- Master Limited Partnerships (MLPs)
- Buy-Write (also known as Covered Calls) strategy

Fixed Income Portfolio

For the fixed income part, I wanted bonds from different classes as follows:

- General bonds (go anywhere bond funds)
- Senior loans (also known as floating rate loans)
- Emerging market fixed income
- Convertible securities
- High yield bonds

Components of Sleep Soundly CEF Portfolio

I selected one CEF from each of the ten different asset classes described above. For this portfolio, rather than using a 3 year look-back period, I chose only funds that had been in existence during the 2008 bear market so that I could judge performance over a complete bear-bull cycle. Thus I began with a long 7 year look-back (October, 2007 to October 2014). If the portfolio looked good over the whole period, I would then check to see how well the portfolio did over more recent periods.

There is no precise way to select different CEFs for inclusion in the portfolio. I used some of my articles written on http://www.seekingalpha.com and on http://www.superchargeretirementincome.com to build a list of candidates. I then ran these candidates through the correlation and risk/reward filters discussed in previous chapter. The CEFs that I picked are summarized below. Note that some of these funds have already been described in earlier chapter but some of the information will be repeated here for convenience.

Gabelli Equity Trust (GAB): I wanted to have one pure equity play in my portfolio since the overall market has been extremely strong and I wanted to capture some of the upside potential if the bull continued to run. Due to its first-class performance, this CEF typically sells at a premium between 2% and 4%. This fund utilizes a strict value methodology and has been managed by the founder, Mario Gabelli, since its inception in 1986. Mr. Gabelli also owns, directly or indirectly, about 1.6 million shares of the fund. The fund has about 400 holdings, with about 82% invested in North America and the rest primarily in Europe. It uses 20% leverage and has an expense ratio of 1.4%. The distribution rate is usually about 8%, which is funded by income, realized capital gains, and Return of Capital (ROC). The ROC is not considered destructive since it comes primarily from unrealized capital gains.

John Hancock Premium Dividend Fund (PDT). Preferred stock funds are generally less volatile than their common stock cousins. As long as interest rates are low, preferred stocks should perform well. Preferred stocks were described in Chapter 2. This John Hancock fund contains 70% preferred stock with the remainder of the portfolio invested in dividend-paying equities. It typically sells at a discount between 6% and 11%. The fund usually has a distribution of about 7%, none of which comes from ROC. It has over 100 holdings, with the utility sector accounting for almost half of the total assets. The fund uses 34% leverage and has an expense ratio of 1.8% (including interest payments).

Eaton Vance Tax-Managed Buy-Write Opportunities Fund (ETV). Covered call (also called buy-write) funds sell options to enhance their return. This should provide some protection in a down market while delivering reasonable appreciation when the market moves higher. Covered call funds are described in Chapter 9. This CEF typically sells at a discount between 3% and 8%. This is a large fund with over 200 holdings, all from the United States. About 60% of the holdings are from S&P 500 stocks and the other 40% are from NASDAQ stocks. The name "tax-managed" means that the fund managers try to minimize the tax burden by periodically selling stocks that have incurred losses and replacing them with similar holdings. This strategy has the effect of reducing or delaying taxable gains. The fund writes options on 84% of the portfolio. The fund does not use leverage and has an expense ratio of 1.1%. The distribution is usually about 8% to 9%, funded primarily by non-destructive ROC.

Cohen and Steers REIT and Preferred Fund (RNP). Historically, Real Estate Investment Trusts (REITs) have been a favorite asset class for income oriented investors. REITs were hit hard in the 2008 bear market, but have rebounded strongly along with other equities since 2009. One of the reasons REITs are so popular is that they receive special tax treatment and as a result, are required to distribute at least 90% of their taxable income each year. REITs are described in Chapter 10. This CEF has about 200 holdings consisting of a combination of both REITs (51%) and preferred stocks (47%). It typically sells for a discount between 9% and 12%. The fund uses 29% leverage and has an expense ratio of 1.8%, including interest payments. The distribution is usually about 7%, consisting primarily of income with some non-destructive ROC.

Kayne Anderson MLP Investment (KYN). Master Limited Partnerships (MLPs) are a unique asset class known for their high yields. Like REITs, MLPs must distribute a large portion of their income. Most MLPs operate in the "midstream" portion of the energy production cycle which involves the storing, transporting, or processing of energy (as opposed to "upstream" exploration or "downstream" retail sales). Therefore, they are relatively insensitive to many of the economic forces that affect other assets. MLPs are described in more details in Chapter 11. This CEF is structured as a C-corporation and typically sells for a premium of between 5% and 8%. It holds about 70 MLP securities and uses 32% leverage. The expense ratio is 2.6%, including interest. The distribution is usually around 6% consisting of income and non-destructive ROC.

PIMCO Income Opportunity Fund (PKO). This is a go-anywhere income fund that has the flexibility to build a portfolio consisting of PIMCO's best ideas, including global bonds, bank loans, and sovereign debt. This CEF typically sells for a premium between 3% and 4%. This fund has more than $500 million in assets and is managed by Dan Ivascyn. The portfolio has about 480 holdings, allocated primarily among asset-backed bonds (49%), corporate bonds (33%) and government bonds (16%). Only about 30% of the holdings are investment grade. The fund utilizes 38% leverage and has an expense ratio of 1.9%. The distribution is usually around 8%, with no ROC.

Western Asset Emerging Markets Debt Fund (ESD). Emerging markets refer to securities domiciled in a country considered to be emerging from an under-developed economy to a more mainstream environment. I selected an emerging market bonds fund for the portfolio because 1) they generally offer higher yields than comparable bonds from developed countries and 2) because the prices of these bonds rise and fall due to local conditions, which may not be in sync with U.S. markets. This CEF typically sells at a discount between 7% and 10%. It has about 200 holdings with about 50% in sovereign debt and 44% in corporate bonds. The assets are distributed among several countries, including Mexico (9%), Turkey (8%), Indonesia (8%), Venezuela (7%), Russia (7%), and Brazil (7%). The fund uses only 8% leverage and has an expense ratio of 1%. This distribution rate is usually around 8% with no ROC.

Invesco Credit Opportunities Fund (VTA). This fund invests in floating-rate loans from both the U.S. (60%) and Europe (40%). This provides the portfolio with a hedge against rising rates since the interest rates associated with floating-rate loans are adjustable. This CEF typically sells for a discount between 5% and 8%. It usually has a distribution of about 7%, none of which is ROC. The fund has about 550 holdings, with 78% in floating-rate loans and the rest primarily in high-yield corporate bonds. VTA utilizes 31% leverage and has an expense ratio of 2.2%, including interest payments

Calamos Convertible Opportunities and Income Fund (CHI). A "convertible security" is an investment, usually a bond or preferred stock that can be converted into a company's common stock. The attraction of convertible CEFs is that they offer upside potential with some protection on the downside. This CEF typically sells for a small premium of about 1%. The fund has 280 holdings with 61% in convertibles and the 36% in corporate bonds (mostly high yield). The fund utilizes 28% leverage and has an expense ratio of 1.5%. The distribution is usually about 8%, comprised of income and non-destructive return of capital.

Western Asset High Income Opportunities Fund (HIO). This fund invests in "high yield" or "junk" bonds. These are bonds that have been rated "below investment grade" by the bond rating agencies. As the name implies, these bonds offer higher yields due to their increased risk of default. In addition to sensitivity to interest rates, high yield bonds prices also follow the ups and downs of the economic cycles (similar to equities). This fund typically sells at discount between 1% and 8%. The distribution rate is usually about 7% with no ROC. The fund has about 400 holdings, most of which are high yield bonds rated between BB and CCC. This is a global fund with only 5% of the holding domiciled within the USA. This fund does not use leverage and has a low expense rate of 0.9%.

Sleep Soundly CEF Portfolio

If you equal weight each of the selected CEFs, the resulting portfolio will typically have an average distribution of between 7% and 8%, so it certainly meets my criteria for high income. Since this portfolio has about 50% equities (assuming REITs and MLP are categorized as equities) and 50% fixed income, you might expect that the portfolio's volatility and return would be significantly less than the S&P 500. To determine if this expectation was borne out by the data, I included the S&P 500 ETF (SPY) as my benchmark:

To assess the performance of the Sleep Soundly Portfolio, I plotted the annualized rate of return in excess of the risk free rate (called Excess Mu in the charts) versus the volatility of each of the component funds from October 12, 2007 (the market high before the bear market collapse) until October 10, 2014. This plot that is shown in Figure 15-1.

The plot illustrates that the CEF components have booked a wide range of returns and volatilities since 2007. To better assess the relative performance of these funds, I calculated the Sharpe Ratio. In Figure 1, I plotted a line that represents the Sharpe Ratio associated with SPY. If an asset is above the line, it has a higher Sharpe Ratio than SPY. Conversely, if an asset is below the line, the reward-to-risk is worse than SPY.

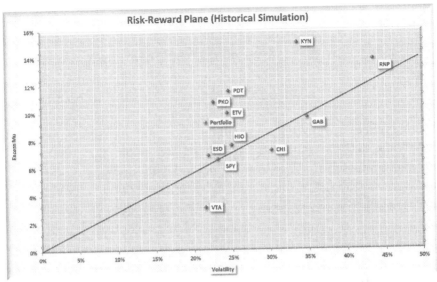

Figure 15-1. Risk versus reward CEF portfolio over the bear-bull cycle.

Some interesting observations are evident from the figure.

- Over the complete cycle, most of the selected CEFs were volatile, but also provided high returns resulting in a risk-adjusted performance that handily beat the S&P 500.
- The bond CEFs (VTA, ESD, and PKO) were the least volatile. PKO had the best performance beating the S&P 500 on both an absolute and risk-adjusted basis. The covered call CEF (PDT) and the MLP CEF (KYN) also had excellent performance similar to PKO.
- The floating rate CEF (VTA) lagged badly over the bear-bull cycle. This is likely because interest rates were kept low by the Federal Reserve, which put pressure on floating rate instruments.
- The convertible CEF was more volatile than SPY and lagged in risk-adjusted performance.
- The three most volatile CEFs (KYN, GAB, and RNP) also had high returns resulting in a risk-adjusted performance better than SPY.

Dr. John Dowdee

- On a risk-adjusted basis, the best performing CEFs in order were PKO, PDT, KYN, and ETV.

I then combined these 10 CEFs into an equally weighted Sleep Soundly Portfolio and assessed how the combined portfolio performed. The risk versus reward of the combined portfolio is shown as a "dot" labeled "portfolio" on the figure. As you can see, the combined portfolio had a volatility less than most of the constituent volatilities. This is an illustration of Markowitz's amazing discovery that was discussed in Chapter 8 that said that the key to constructing a lower volatility portfolio was to select components not highly correlated with one another.

To verify that the selected CEFs did in fact have low correlations, I calculated the correlation matrix for the CEFs (and SPY) over the 7 year period. The results are shown in Figure 15-2. Among the CEFs, all the correlations were relatively small (in the 40% to 60% range). These results are consistent with a well-diversified portfolio.

Correlation Matrix										
	CHI	ESD	ETV	GAB	HIO	KYN	PDT	PKO	RNP	VTA	SPY
CHI	1.000										
ESD	0.360	1.000									
ETV	0.522	0.378	1.000								
GAB	0.436	0.328	0.620	1.000							
HIO	0.365	0.418	0.370	0.340	1.000						
KYN	0.276	0.275	0.385	0.313	0.228	1.000					
PDT	0.368	0.398	0.458	0.345	0.323	0.318	1.000				
PKO	0.369	0.472	0.375	0.357	0.383	0.252	0.364	1.000			
RNP	0.449	0.438	0.544	0.448	0.403	0.289	0.428	0.413	1.000		
VTA	0.389	0.406	0.451	0.370	0.319	0.259	0.319	0.391	0.343	1.000	
SPY	0.491	0.303	0.788	0.682	0.321	0.352	0.407	0.306	0.539	0.348	1.000

Figure 15-2. Correlation matrix of CEF Portfolio over the bear-bull cycle.

This portfolio would also work well in conjunction with a more general portfolio that mimics the S&P 500. The covered call fund (PDT), the REIT fund (RNP), and the equity fund (GAB) were all moderately correlated with the S&P 500. The other CEFs were much less correlated with SPY.

My next step was to assess this portfolio over a shorter time frame when the S&P 500 was in a strong bull market. I chose a look-back period of 3 years, from October 2011 to October 2014. The data is shown in Figure 15-3 and as you might anticipate, during this bull market period, the SPY outperformed most of the CEFs. Only the covered call fund (ETV) was able to keep pace with SPY on a risk-adjusted basis. The individual components continued to be volatile but the portfolio had volatility about 30% less than SPY. It is true that the portfolio gave up some absolute return with respect to the S&P 500 but it was also significantly safer. On a risk-adjusted basis, the portfolio actually beat the S&P 500 by a small amount.

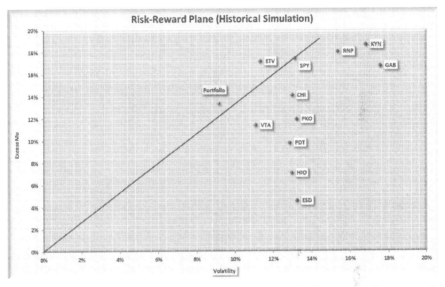

Figure 15-3. Risk versus reward CEF portfolio over the past 3 years.

Summary CEF Portfolio

No one knows what the future will hold but this portfolio satisfied our criteria for high income and low risk over the look-back periods. Some attributes of this portfolio are summarized below.

- The Sleep Soundly CEF Portfolio has generated greater return with lower risk than the S&P 500 over the bear-bull cycle beginning in 2007.

- The Sleep Soundly CEF Portfolio outperformed the S&P 500 on a risk-adjusted basis for all time frames analyzed since 2007.
- The Sleep Soundly Portfolio provides over 7.5% income and still allows me to sleep soundly each night.

Chapter 16
Sleep Soundly ETF Portfolio

The previous chapter showed how to construct a Sleep Soundly Portfolio with actively managed Closed End Funds (CEFs). However, some investors prefer to use ETFs that track passive indexes. This chapter constructs a Sleep Soundly Portfolio using ETFs and then compares the risk and reward associated with the two portfolios.

As a quick recap, the following assets classes were used to construct the portfolio

For the equity portion, I wanted to select representatives from the following asset classes:

Equity Portion of Portfolio
- General equity
- Preferred stocks
- Real Estate Investment Trusts (REITS)
- Master Limited Partnerships (MLPs)
- Buy-Write (also known as Covered Calls) strategy

Fixed Income Portion of Portfolio
- General bonds (go anywhere bond funds)
- Senior loans (also known as floating rate loans)
- Emerging market fixed income
- Convertible securities
- High yield bonds.

Constructing an ETF Portfolio

In the previous chapter, I selected one CEF to represent each asset class. In this chapter, I will select an ETF for each asset class. A major difference between ETFs and CEFs is that CEFs are actively managed while ETFs are usually passive and track a predefined index.

In addition, CEFs are allowed to use leverage while ETFs are typically unleveraged investments. In general, I chose some of the most liquid ETFs that had at least a 3 year history (since some of the ETFs did not have sufficient history to go back to 2007). These ETFs are summarized below. As in the last chapter, some of the tutorial material is repeated for convenience.

SPDR S&P 500 (SPY). This ETF is representative of the general equity asset class and tracks the S&P 500 index. It is one of the most liquid ETF, trading on average over 80 million shares per day. This index is cap weighted and measures the performance of large and mid-cap stocks. It has an expense ratio of 0.09% and typically yields about 1.8%.

iShares US Preferred Stock (PFF). Preferred stock funds are generally less volatile than their common stock cousins. As long as interest rates are low, preferred stocks should perform well. This ETF tracks 284 preferred stocks on the New York Stock Exchange and the NASDAQ. About 87% of the preferred stocks are from financial institutions such as banks and insurance companies. This ETF has an expense ratio of 0.47% and typically yields about 6.7%.

Vanguard REIT (VNQ). Historically, Real Estate Investment Trusts (REITs) have been a favorite asset class for income oriented investors. One of the reasons REITs are so popular is that they receive special tax treatment and as a result, are required to distribute at least 90% of their taxable income each year. This ETF tracks a cap weighted index of 120 REITs, all domiciled in the U.S. The fund's expense ratio is 0.10% and the typically yields about 3%.

Alerian MLP (AMLP). Master Limited Partnerships (MLPs) are a unique asset class known for their high yields. This ETF tracks an index of 25 MLPs. The ETF is structured as a C-corporation and has to pay corporate income tax but on the plus side, most of the distribution is treated as return of capital due to large depreciation of MLP assets. The yield is usually about 5.8%.

PowerShares S&P 500 BuyWrite (PBP). Covered call (also called buy-write) funds sell options to enhance their return. This should provide some protection in a down market while delivering reasonable appreciation when the market moves higher. This ETF is designed to mimic the performance of writing one-month, at-the-money index options against the S&P 500. The fund holds the stocks of the S&P 500 as well as options. Because of the portfolio construction, the ETF is about 87% correlated with SPY. PBP has an expense ratio of 0.75% and the yield is usually around 6.8%.

iShares Core US Aggregate Bond (AGG). This ETF is representative of the general bond asset class and holds over 2,000 bonds across all maturities. The largest constituents of the portfolio are US government bonds (43%) followed by mortgage backed securities at 27% and investment grade corporate bonds at 21%. The expense ratio is 0.08% and the yield is typically about 2.2%.

PowerShares Senior Loans (BKLN). Senior loans are loans made to below investment grade companies to support business purposes, such as expansion. The loans are typically large, with sizes in the $50 million to over a billion dollar range. They are called "senior" loans because they are backed by real assets and are the first to be paid when a company pays its debts. The loans are also known as "floating rate" because the rate of interest is adjustable and moves higher or lower based on a benchmark, usually the London Interbank Offer Rate (Libor). This ETF contains 100 securities associated with the largest institutional leverage loans. This ETF was launched in March of 2011 so this limits the look-back period to about 3.5 years. The fund has an expense ratio of 0.65% and the yield is about 4%.

PowerShares Emerging Market Sovereign Debt (PCY). Emerging markets refer to securities domiciled in a country considered to be emerging from an under-developed economy to a more mainstream environment. Emerging market bonds generally offer higher yields than comparable bonds from developed countries and their prices rise and fall due to local conditions, which may not be in sync with U.S. markets. The portfolio of this ETF consists of 60 sovereign bonds (priced in US dollars so there is no foreign currency exposure) from 22 different countries. The bonds are selected to achieve equal weights for each country. The expense ratio is 0.5% and yield is about 4.3%.

SPDR Barclays Convertible Securities (CWB). A "convertible security" is an investment, usually a bond or preferred stock, which can be converted into a company's common stocks. The attraction of convertibles securities is that they offer upside potential with some protection on the downside. This fund is the only ETF that invests exclusively in convertible securities. It has 96 holdings with about 40% rated as investment grade. The fund has an expense ratio of 0.4% and yield is usually around 3.2%.

iShares iBoxx $ High Yield Corporate Bonds (HYG). As the name implies, these bonds offer higher yields due to their increased risk of default. They are also called "junk bonds". In addition to sensitivity to interest rates, high yield bonds prices also follow the ups and downs of the economic cycles (similar to equities). This ETF has about 900 holdings and is diversified across all sectors of the market. Bonds from the consumer discretionary sector makes up the largest component of the portfolio at 16%. The fund has an expense ratio of 0.5% and yield is typically about 5.7%.

Sleep Soundly ETF Portfolio

If you equal weight the above ETFs, the resulting portfolio has a yield of about 4% to 5%, which is good but still much lower than the 7% to 8% distribution associated with the CEF portfolio. However, to most investors, total return and risk are just as important as yield so I plotted the annualized rate of return in excess of the risk free rate (called Excess Mu in the charts) versus the volatility of each of the component ETFs. Unfortunately, many of the ETFs were launched after the 2008 bear market so I could not assess performance during a severe downturn. I used October, 2011 as my starting point so I only used a 3 year look-back period for this portfolio (end date was October, 2014). Figure 15-1 provides the results for the ETF portfolio over the past 3 years.

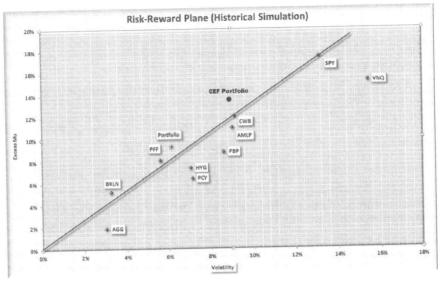

Figure 16-1. Risk versus reward ETF Portfolio over past 3 years

The plot illustrates that the ETFs components have booked a wide range of returns and volatilities. To better assess the relative performance of these funds, I calculated the Sharpe Ratio. In Figure 1, I plotted a line that represents the Sharpe Ratio associated with SPY. If an asset is above the line, it has a higher Sharpe Ratio than SPY. Conversely, if an asset is below the line, the reward-to-risk is worse than SPY.

Some observations are evident from the figure.

- With the exception of VNQ, all the ETFs are substantially less volatile than the S&P 500.
- The S&P 500 had the best absolute return and one of the best risk-adjusted return (BKLN and PFF were only slightly better on a risk-adjusted basis).
- The REIT ETF (VNQ) had the highest volatility coupled with the second highest absolute return. However, on a risk-adjusted basis, VNQ placed in the middle of the pack.
- As you might expect, AGG had the lowest volatility and this was coupled with a relatively low absolute return. On a risk-adjusted basis, AGG lagged the SPY.

I then combined these 10 ETFs into an equally weighted Sleep Soundly Portfolio and assessed how the combined portfolio performed. The risk versus reward of the combined portfolio is shown as a "dot" called "Portfolio" on the figure. As you can see, the combined portfolio had a volatility that was less than most of the constituent volatilities. As discussed in the previous chapter as well as Chapter 8, this is an illustration of Modern Portfolio Theory as developed by Markowitz.

The other dot, called CEF Portfolio, represents the risk versus reward associated with the CEF portfolio constructed in Chapter 15. As expected, the ETF portfolio had lower volatility as well as lower return. However, on a risk-adjusted basis, the performance of the ETF portfolio was similar to the CEF portfolio. Thus you could choose either of these portfolios depending on your risk tolerance.

To conclude the analysis, I also computed the pair-wise correlations for the ETFs. This is shown in Figure 16-2 based on a 3 year look-back period. Most of the constituent ETFs had low to moderately correlations with each other. The exceptions were AGG, which has a low to negative correlation with most of the other ETFs and SPY, which was highly correlated with CWB and PBP. These results are consistent with a well-diversified portfolio.

Correlation Matrix	AGG	AMLP	BKLN	CWB	HYG	PBP	PCY	PFF	SPY	VNQ
AGG	1.000	0.07	0.02	-0.15	0.17	-0.16	0.30	0.28	-0.18	0.20
AMLP	0.069	1.000	0.27	0.47	0.42	0.40	0.19	0.26	0.45	0.33
BKLN	0.021	0.274	1.000	0.33	0.37	0.29	0.16	0.21	0.33	0.17
CWB	-0.148	0.468	0.333	1.000	0.60	0.77	0.22	0.38	0.87	0.50
HYG	0.173	0.420	0.368	0.600	1.000	0.59	0.40	0.51	0.66	0.50
PBP	-0.176	0.401	0.293	0.772	0.602	1.000	0.18	0.34	0.88	0.51
PCY	0.301	0.192	0.158	0.215	0.405	0.180	1.000	0.34	0.23	0.32
PFF	0.275	0.255	0.211	0.375	0.513	0.340	0.339	1.000	0.36	0.41
SPY	-0.183	0.451	0.334	0.867	0.659	0.877	0.227	0.362	1.000	0.58
VNQ	0.205	0.329	0.169	0.504	0.497	0.509	0.322	0.414	0.580	1.000

Figure 16-2. Correlation matrix ETF Portfolio since March 2011

Summary of ETF Portfolio

The Sleep Soundly ETF Portfolio is less volatile than the CEF Portfolio but also provides less return. The portfolio outperformed the S&P 500 on a risk-adjusted basis for all time frames analyzed since 2011. However, on a risk-adjusted basis, the ETF and CEF Sleep Soundly Portfolios had almost identical performance.

Chapter 17
Parting Thoughts

The CEF and ETF portfolios had virtually the same risk-adjusted performance over the time periods analyzed. These are examples of how to construct a unique portfolio that is consistent with you risk profile. Based on my risk profile, I am pleased with the performances of both these portfolio and have personally invested in them but each investor must assess their own risk profile and investment objectives.

These portfolios were only examples and I make no forecast as to how either of these portfolios might perform in the future. If you are risk adverse, you might be better served by selecting the ETF portfolio. However, if you can tolerate the higher risk, the CEF portfolio might be a better choice.

I would not expect either of these portfolios to perform well in a major bear market so they are not "buy and forget" investments. There will times when you need to rotate out of some assets and move into others. There will be times to circle your wagons and times to be aggressive. Unlike most authors, I believe tactical portfolio management is the best way to go. To protect yourself when the market goes south, you will need to implement proactive risk management techniques. The sequel to this book will discuss how to "crash proof" your portfolio based on technical analysis and the use of options. However, as long as the market fluctuations are not too severe, either of these portfolios should allow most investors to sleep soundly each night.

If you enjoyed this book, please let me know by sending an email to DrD@superchargeretirmentincome.com. If you have suggestions for improvement, I would love to hear them. Also, if you have time, I would greatly appreciate if you could write a review on the website where you purchased the book. I have learned that the best way to sell books is by word of mouth from satisfied readers. I thank you in advance.

Best of luck in the coming years and may your years be productive and prosperous.

22743620R00098

Made in the USA
Middletown, DE
07 August 2015